The Vikings and their Origins

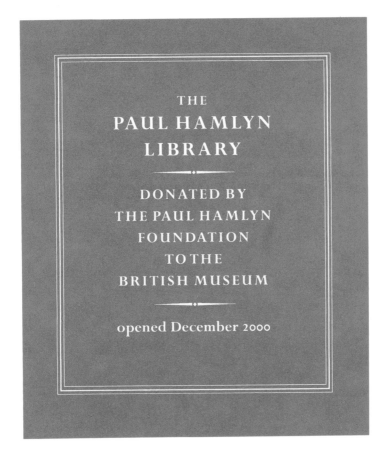

DAVID M. WILSON

The Vikings
and their Origins

SCANDINAVIA
IN THE FIRST MILLENNIUM

Thames & Hudson

On the cover: *Detail of the hilt and upper part of a rich sixth-century sword from grave V at Snartemo, Hägebostad, Vest Agder, Norway*

First published in the United Kingdom in 1970 by Thames & Hudson Ltd, 181A High Holborn, London WC1V 7QX

© 1970 and 1989 Thames & Hudson Ltd, London
Reprinted 1999

British Library Cataloguing-in-Publication Data
A catalogue record for this book is available from the British Library
ISBN 0-500-27542-4

Printed and bound in Singapore by C.S. Graphics

Contents

Preface to revised edition

This book is intended not only to portray an image of the Vikings but to show something of the culture of the Scandinavian countries in which they were settled in the four centuries before they burst on the European scene. The Viking phenomenon has been much written about in the twenty-odd years since this book was first published, but the culture of the Scandinavian people in the period before the Viking incursion has received little attention in the English language. This book is, therefore, still of value in providing a general introduction to one of the most important European movements of the Middle Ages. It has been updated in detail but the main thrust remains, I believe, valid.

In the preface to the first edition, David Talbot-Rice, the general editor, made the point that the Vikings did not create a civilization although they contributed to the general culture of Europe. This is a valid argument and one that needs stressing. The Scandinavians of the Viking Age added to the tapestry of European life in many ways, but did not impose on it the stifling constraints of some of the cultures that appear to the classically-oriented to be of a higher nature. Rather they influenced the life and thought of the whole of Northern and Western Europe and enriched it greatly.

The British Isles received the greatest attention from the Vikings. The North Sea was a Scandinavian ocean at this time and it is rational that the British should be fascinated by these strange people. The English language, for example, is full of words which have Scandinavian roots. The word 'law' is of Scandinavian origin, as is the word 'starboard' and half a hundred nautical terms; so too is 'Tuesday'. Such basic terminology is often instanced as illustrating the enormous influence of the Vikings on England. But then the word 'husband' has a Scandinavian root and one cannot pretend that this is of any deep historical or philosophical meaning. What we should be saying is that the Scandinavians passed this way and left their mark on the English language. They also left their mark on the English countryside through the place-names: the names Derby and Whitby, for example, are of Danish origin (the termination -by meaning 'a farmstead' or 'village': thus Derby is 'settlement with deer' and Whitby is 'the white farm').

The story told in this book is based largely on evidence taken from archaeology. Excavations and casual finds in all the Scandinavian countries, as well as in those countries in which they settled, in the period between 800 and 1100 (when the Vikings were at their most active) tell in some detail of the day-to-day life of the Vikings. They tell of their funerary practices, their houses and (increasingly) their villages, their first towns, their first faltering steps along the road to literacy and their conversion from paganism to Christianity. By means of standing monuments and in their jewellery we gain an insight into their art, through patterns which tease the eye and show at once that Scandinavians were in the mainstream of the Germanic ornamental tradition and that their sturdy independence resisted any great artistic influence from outside. It is perhaps in this material that we catch the clearest glimpse of the continuity of Scandinavian culture from the fifth to the eleventh centuries: for it tells the story of the development of a small corpus of ornamental motifs.

Their literature for this period is largely missing. A few long inscriptions on tenth- and eleventh-century stone monuments hint at considerable technical skill in prose and verse. The histories, stories and poems enshrined in the Eddaic literature and in the sagas were, with few exceptions, all written down long after the last Viking king had withdrawn from England, after the last settlement in the Atlantic islands and after the last raids into continental Europe. Yet these stories – much overlaid by Christian tradition – can at least help us to grope for the minds of these pagan northern barbarians. Such traces of their lost literature perhaps deny Talbot-Rice's assertion that the Vikings lacked that 'touch of humanism' which is the hallmark of civilization.

Let us not, however, split hairs. The Vikings were barbarians, cruel and brutal. But they had such attributes in an age when barbarism, cruelty and brutality was not confined to pagan illiterates. Charlemagne himself – the model of wisdom, valour and Christian virtue – was capable of acts in every way as brutal to modern eyes as those perpetrated by the Vikings; consider for example the baptisms which he forced on the Saxon people after he had destroyed the sacred Irminsul – the great tree trunk which according to the Saxons supported the heavens – or the massacre of 4500 prisoners after the victory near Verden in 782.

In today's terminology the Scandinavians of the Viking Age have had a bad press because the people who were writing about them – namely the literate Christians of the

West – were largely the people who were being attacked by them. It is not correct, however, to paint the Scandinavians in either black or white; like most people they were grey. Their strength lay in their trading activities, in their ability to settle new lands, to fight bravely and to test the unknown. They were no mean, destructive people: rather people of wide vision who were to make a considerable contribution to European wholeness once they had become Christian and had settled down to become the nations which we know to-day.

Introduction to first edition

The Vikings were one of the most remarkable pheno-
mena ever to burst on the European scene. Suddenly,
apparently out of nowhere, waves of raiders appeared
along the coastline of Western Europe. 'Never before',
wrote Alcuin, the leading scholar of Europe, in 793, 'has
such terror appeared in Britain as we have now suffered
from a pagan race, nor was it thought that such an inroad
from the sea could be made. Behold the church of St
Cuthbert spattered with the blood of the priests of God,
despoiled of all its ornaments; a place more venerable
than all in Britain is given as a prey to pagan peoples.'
The shock of this attack has burnt itself into the minds of
European historians and scholars, many of whom to this
day echo Alcuin's words and thoughts. But the Viking
attacks do not reflect the situation in Scandinavia itself.
For many Scandinavians who lived in the homeland
throughout this traumatic period of their people's
history, society and daily life did not change in any very
marked fashion. The basic economy of Scandinavia was
still, as it had been from the beginning of the millennium,
pastoral or agrarian. It is my intention in this book to
outline the Viking adventure against the background of
the Scandinavians in their homeland. The development
seen in Scandinavian society from the birth of Christ to
the end of the Viking Age, about 1100, is a continuous
one – the gradual emergence of a group of pagan tribes
into a Christian community accepted by its peers in
Western Europe. The adventures of the Vikings in
Russia, Ireland, England, America and Byzantium –

important though they may be – are incidental to this process. Christianity and its concomitant, literacy, was the catalyst which finally accomplished the change.

A book of this length, expanded from a single chapter of the parent volume which dealt with the whole of the Western world of the first millennium AD, cannot be more than a sketch of a people living in a vast tract of country at a time of great political, economic and religious change over a period of about a thousand years. It is intended to introduce the general reader to a most fascinating period in the history of Scandinavia – a period represented in the archaeological record by outstanding and beautiful finds and revealed to our eye in some cases by the most advanced archaeological techniques.

In writing this book I have relied to a great extent on many friends in the Scandinavian countries who have discussed the various problems of the period with me and allowed me to study material and collections in their care. Particularly I value many years of friendship with my teacher, the late Holger Arbman, professor of prehistoric and medieval archaeology in the University of Lund, who was perhaps the greatest Viking archaeologist of his generation. To his memory I dedicate this small offering.

D.M.W.

Chapter One

The Unveiling of Scandinavia

Scandinavia is a vast area: a straight line drawn from
southern Jutland to the northernmost point of Norway
would measure some twelve hundred miles in length, a
distance greater than that between southern Jutland and *Ill. 1*
Rome. The southernmost part of Scandinavia lies on the
same latitude as Newcastle; North Cape in Norway lies
235 miles north of the Arctic Circle. The area is united
nowadays by its people, its blood-ties and its geographical situation as the north-western corner of Europe. Physi-
cally it is united only by the sea; the lush pastures of
Jutland, the rich farm lands of Skåne and South Norway,
bear little relationship to the high fells of Norway or the
forests of Swedish Småland. The variation in climate is
enormous and the natural economy varies accordingly.

The Classical Sources

This vast area was hardly known to the Roman world at
the beginning of our era. Pytheas, three hundred years
earlier, had described – albeit at second hand – what must
be Norway to the sceptical scientists of the Mediterranean.
He labelled it *Thule*, where, 'for lack of the crops and
cattle of more genial lands, its inhabitants subsist on wild
berries and "millet" which they thresh in covered barns
because of the continual rains. From the plentiful honey
of their bees they prepare mead as a drink.' Many of his
contemporaries and successors did not believe Pytheas,
but gradually more information began to filter through
to the classical world and so to posterity. The Romans
came into direct contact with the Scandinavians in AD 5

when a Roman fleet made a reconnaissance to the Skaw, the northernmost tip of Jutland. Pliny the Elder, Tacitus and Ptolemy mention several tribes in this area, including the *Suiones*, who must almost certainly be the Swedes (*Svíar*) of Uppland who were to become the richest tribe in Scandinavia and whose territory was to be the kernel of the modern Swedish kingdom. Tacitus tells us that:

> The shape of their ships differs from the normal in having a prow at both ends, they do not rig sails or fasten their oars in banks at the side. . . . Wealth, too, is held in high honour and that is why they obey one rule, with no restrictions on his [the ruler's] authority and with no mere casual claim to obedience. Arms are not, as in the rest of Germany, allowed to all and sundry, but are kept under guard, and the guard is a slave.

At a later date Ptolemy, who wrote in Egypt about A D 150, named a number of tribes including the *Goutoi* (who are almost certainly the *Gautar* – the *Geatas* of the great Anglo-Saxon epic *Beowulf*) and the *Chaideinoi* (who are probably to be identified with the Norwegian *Heidnir*).

For nearly three hundred years the Scandinavians pass out of literature and, since they were themselves to all intents illiterate, our knowledge of them must rest on the vast corpus of archaeological remains meticulously excavated by Scandinavian scholars in the last 150 years. It is

1 Map of sites mentioned in the text. NORWAY: 1 Sætrang, 2 Kvalsund, 3 Raknehaugen, ▷ 4 Snartemo, 5 Gokstad, 6 Oseberg, 7 Tune, 8 Asker, 9 Kaupang, 10 Borre, 11 Urnes. DENMARK: 12 Hoby, 13 Himmlingøje, 14 Nørre Fjand, 15 Dalshøj, 16 Ginderup, 17 Nydam, 18 Vimose, 19 Ejsbøl, 20 Kragehul, 21 Thorsbjerg, 22 Illerup, 23 Lousgård, 24 Sorte Muld, 25 Lindholm, 26 Trelleborg, 27 Fyrkat, 28 Aggersborg, 29 Jelling. SWEDEN: 30 Fycklinge, 31 Hablingbo, 32 Moos, 33 Kylver, 34 Käringsjön, 35 Skedemosse, 36 Timboholm, 37 Vendel, 38 Valsgärde, 39 Lackalänge, 40 Helgö, 41 Birka, 42 Gråborg, 43 Ismantorp, 44 Eketorp, 45 Vallhagar, 46 Galtabäck, 47 Falsterbo, 48 Västergarn. GERMANY: 49 Hedeby. LATVIA: 50 Grobin.

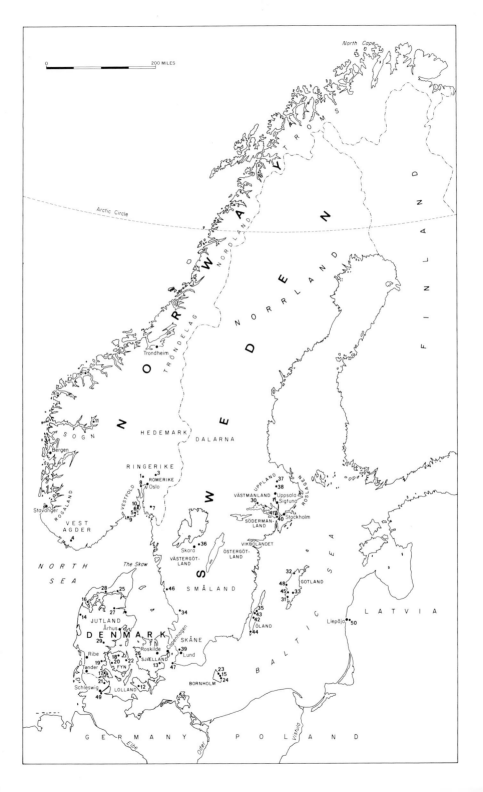

remarkable that the Romans never tried to conquer the Scandinavian tribes, but it seems likely that after the crushing defeat of Varus at the hands of the *Teutones* in AD 9 the Romans decided not to attempt the conquest of a distant land, the tribes of which were apparently permanently locked in internecine war: political and military considerations apparently outweighed the obvious economic potential of the North. Trade with the North was, however, encouraged and, until the frontiers of the Roman Empire exploded in the third century, trade flowed to the mutual advantage of both Scandinavia and Rome.

The Roman Iron Age

Although archaeological evidence is the main source of knowledge of the first four hundred years of our era in Scandinavia, the dominating influence of a literate empire has caused the period to be labelled 'the Roman Iron Age'. The label is justified if only because exotic goods originating in the Roman Empire form the most obtrusive element in the rich archaeology of southern Scandinavia. Much of this material came to Scandinavia by means of trade – an activity which was not new to the Scandinavians who for many years had had a lively commercial contact with southern Europe.

Most of the imported objects found in Scandinavia come from grave-finds and it is a fortunate coincidence that at this period, in the richer parts of Scandinavia at *Ill. 2* least, the rite of inhumation gradually replaced the hitherto prevailing rite of cremation. The reason for this basic change is not known, but it may have been due in part to contact with the religion of the inhabitants of Silesia and Central Europe. The new rite enables archaeologists to gain a more complete view of the material culture and economy of the Scandinavian people through studying the objects which accompanied the dead to the grave.

2 Female skeleton from a rich grave in the cemetery at Juellinge, on the Danish island of Lolland. On her finger is a gold ring and under her chin, as though clasped by her hand, is an imported Roman sieve. She wore three brooches and had two long pins on either side of her skull, presumably fastening a kerchief in position

Inhumation, however, was not universal; cremation and inhumation burials occasionally occur alongside each other, while cremation was still particularly favoured in Norway, where cemeteries of upwards of a thousand graves have been recorded. The Roman objects found in the inhumation graves are mainly luxury goods – bronze (and even silver) vessels, glass bowls, brooches, moulded red Samian ware (*terra sigillata*) and the occasional bronze figure of a Roman god.

Ills 3–8

Many of the objects reached Scandinavia by trade routes which were apparently controlled by the *Marcomanni*, a tribe – settled at this period in Bohemia – who acted as middlemen between the Celts, Scandinavians and

Romans. Merchants, leaving the security of the Roman Empire, crossed the Danube between Vienna and Linz, travelled through their territory to the Elbe and the Oder and so to the Baltic and Scandinavia. A secondary trade route led from the mouth of the Rhine, along the Frisian coast to the western seaboard of Scandinavia, and is demonstrated archaeologically by the presence in these areas of Roman silver coins (*denarii*) – a sure clue to the passage of Roman trade. This western route, and an eastern one along the Vistula, were to become much more important later in the Roman period.

The Roman imports found in Scandinavia are, of course, merely fossils of a considerable trade; other goods of a more perishable nature also came from the South but have left no record in the archaeological material. Among these objects of trade must have been silks and other textiles, spices and, almost certainly, wine. That the inhabitants of these cold northern countries had a considerable interest in alcohol is attested by the large number of drinking-vessels, including many drinking-horn mounts, found in the graves. Richer members of the community would presumably have been only too pleased to supplement their native drinks of mead and beer with imported Mediterranean wines.

In return for these luxuries the Scandinavians probably exported goods of the type for which there is literary evidence at a later period – furs, skins, ropes made of sealskin, dairy produce and even cattle. Slaves also were probably one of the most important exports of Scandinavia. Another popular export in both prehistoric and historic times was Baltic amber, a substance which fetched high prices in the Mediterranean. The importance of the amber trade has, however, almost certainly been overemphasized by archaeologists who have been fascinated by the amount of amber found in southern Europe, for some of it is certainly not of Baltic origin.

3 An imported bronze jug decorated with an elegant vine-scroll from the grave at Hoby, which also contained the objects illustrated in *Ill. 4*. At the base of the handle is a figure of Cupid. A Roman object, of the finest Augustan quality, it is the only one of its type found in Denmark

Luxuries from the South

The luxury trade, naturally, makes the greatest impact on the modern eye. Although the perishable goods have disappeared, there are, in the Scandinavian graves, such extraordinary testimonies to the far-flung trading connections of the period as the Danish grave-find of Hoby, on the island of Lolland. Chief amongst the objects buried in this grave are two silver beakers of remarkable quality *Ill. 4* made by a Greek craftsman – Cheirisophos – who must have been active in Rome in the first century AD. The grave also contained a skillet made in Capua and two

4, 5 *Above:* Imported objects from the rich grave at Hoby, Lolland (the jug is also illustrated in *Ill. 3*). The jug and the large dish are of bronze and the two handled cups are of silver. The cups are inscribed on the base with the name of the Greek craftsman who made them, as well as the name of the owner, Silius, and a note of their weight. The scenes depicted on the cups are from the Homeric cycle and among those portrayed are Priam, Achilles, Odysseus, Heracles and Philoctectus. The dish portrays Venus between two cupids. *Left:* Large bronze vessel found in 1819 while levelling a cairn at Fycklinge, Björksta, Västmanland, Sweden. The inscription reads: APOLLINI GRANNO DONUM AMMILIVS CONSTANS PRAEF TEMPLI IPSIVS VSLLM. Originally it had a double handle, but this was lost in antiquity. It is 45 cm. high

6 Bowl of Samian ware (*terra sigillata*) from a grave at Valloby, Sjælland, Denmark. Bowls of this red fabric are common throughout the Roman Empire, but are only rarely found outside its boundaries. This example bears the maker's stamp *Comitialis* on its base; this potter was active towards the end of the second century

bronze vessels of exceptionally high quality, as well as a salver, a dish and a bucket. The silver cups bear Homeric scenes – Priam and Achilles, Odysseus and Philoctectus – a jug is decorated with a vine-scroll, while Venus appears with a group of cupids on the dish. *Ill. 3*

These objects are among the finest Roman products found in Scandinavia; but others, only slightly less impressive, have come from graves and bogs throughout Denmark, in south and central Sweden – particularly in the rich areas of Uppland and Gotland – and to a lesser extent in Norway. At Fycklinge, in Västmanland in central Sweden, for example, was found a most impressive bronze vessel some 50 cm. high. It is inlaid with silver *Ill. 5* and copper and is inscribed 'to Apollo Grannus this gift is offered by the benefactor of the temple Ammillus Constans.' Another bronze vessel, plundered from a temple (probably in Gaul), was found in Vang in Hedemark, Norway; it bears the inscription, 'Aprus and Livertinus gave this vessel to the temple.' Two splendid glass vessels from Himmlingøje, Sjælland, one of which is decorated with a series of coloured animals including a splendid blue leopard, witness to the Scandinavian taste for Roman luxury articles – whether as the products of trade, as loot or as diplomatic gifts.

Ill. 7

But the Himmlingøje grave is one of the later graves of the Roman Iron Age and it is clear that the import trade changed towards the end of the second century, presumably when the Marcomannic kingdom was destroyed after the attack on the Danubian frontier of the Roman Empire in 165 and after the settlement of the frontier by the Goths (who began to control the trade of Central Europe in the course of the third century). From this time forward the quality of the goods imported from the Roman world into Scandinavia declined considerably as the axis of direct trade shifted westwards. Later Roman objects found in Scandinavia were mostly made in the province of Gaul. The mercantile activity which imported material of this character must have been backed by fairly sophisticated trading stations, which may have been of a semi-permanent nature. It has been suggested, for example, that in the fourth century there were minor market-places which dealt in Roman goods in southern Vestfold (in South Norway) which drew on both the Baltic and the North Sea for their goods.

During the whole of the Roman Iron Age there was considerable contact between Scandinavia and the eastern Mediterranean by way of the rivers of Eastern Europe, particularly the Vistula. The routes themselves are not very easy to trace, but the mapping of antiquities does occasionally indicate the areas in the Baltic where the objects eventually emerged. Typical evidence of such contacts are the seven thousand *denarii*, spanning the

7 Three imported Roman glass vessels from graves in Denmark, all decorated with animal friezes. The largest, bearing the figure of a bull, dates from about AD 200, the other two date from the end of the third century

whole of the Roman period, which have been found in Sweden – five thousand of them on the island of Gotland. They probably came thither by way of the Russian and Polish rivers, along which are found a large number of similar hoards. Most of these coins must have come through contact with the Goths – a tribe which may originally have been Scandinavian and which was certainly at one time settled on the South Baltic coast. Its members established themselves on the shores of the Black Sea in the early third century and spread thence into Central Europe. Such coin hoards do not reflect a monetary economy, rather they must be seen as bullion – a symbol and fact of wealth.

Ill. 8   The remarkable treasure from Havor, Hablingbo, Gotland, must also be considered as a reflection of wealth. It was discovered in 1961 within the banks of a fortified encampment and consists of a shouldered bronze pail, 33 cm. high, a matching ladle and strainer (the latter stamped with the maker's name – CANNIMASVIT), three other ladles, two bronze bells and – most remarkable of all – a gold neck-ring more than 24 cm. in diameter, beautifully decorated with filigree. The handle of the pail is supported by cast brackets in the form of human masks. It is of Campanian origin, while the neck-ring must have had its origin in South Russia. It has been suggested that the ring was not intended to be worn by a human, but rather that it adorned an idol, and the excavator of the find has tentatively suggested that the hoard may represent the treasure of a temple. Such an hypothesis is interesting but coincidental to the indications it gives of

8 Bronze Campanian situla found together with a group of imported bronzes and a gold ▷ neck-ring at Havor, Hablingbo, Gotland. The neck-ring is of south Russian origin and is one of the first definite traces of contact with an area which was to become increasingly important to Sweden, and particularly to Gotland, in the course of the first millennium

the trading connections of the Swedes and the wealth of the Scandinavians as revealed by this treasure. Eastern imports have also been encountered in Norway: certain objects in a rich grave of the fourth century from Sætrang, not far from Oslo, have been shown to have come from south-eastern Europe, by way of the Baltic.

The Runes

An element in Scandinavian culture which may have come to Scandinavia by the same route as the gold collar from Havor is literacy, which is first indicated in Scandinavia by the runes, which appear towards the end of the second or at the beginning of the third century of our era. They are first found, for example, on weapons from Moos in Gotland and Stabu, some seventy-five miles north of Oslo, where they presumably spell out the name given to the weapon by its first owner – a practice documented in early Germanic literature. The earliest Scandinavian runic alphabet occurs on a stone of the late fourth or early fifth century from a cist grave at Kylver in Gotland. The first six letters of the inscription give the name – *fuþark* – to the Scandinavian runic alphabet. The main inscription reads *fuþarkgwhnijpëRstbemlngdo*; this is followed by an uninterpretable sign which looks like a fir-tree and, a little above and to the right, the five letters *sueus* (apparently a meaningless word). It can be seen from the *Ill. 9* idealized runic alphabet illustrated that the runic letters were made up in almost every case of straight strokes, ideally suited for carving across the grain of wood or on stone. From the Roman Iron Age onwards this form of writing appears in an unbroken sequence, mostly occurring on objects of stone and wood, right through to the nineteenth century. Wood was the natural medium of this strange alphabet, as is well demonstrated by the vast amount of medieval material found during the excavations at Bergen in Norway, where texts vary from

ᚠᚢᚦᚨᚱᚲᚷᚹ ᚺᚾᛁᛃᛈᛇᛉᛊᛏᛒᛖᛗᛚᛜᛞᛟ

f u þ a r k g w h n i j p e R s t b e m l ng d o

9 The runic alphabet or futhark (the third character has the value 'th') is here shown in one of its earliest forms. It was to be used in the north for more than a thousand years. Originally designed for carving on wood or stone, the angular form of the characters was conditioned by the nature of the material on which they were incised

'lavatory-wall' inscriptions to trading documents and private letters. It is unfortunate that most of the inscriptions that are to be dated within the period covered by this book are on sepulchral or memorial monuments, or on weapons – the wooden evidence has almost completely disappeared.

Runes are widely considered to be endowed with magical significance. That there undoubtedly was a magical or religious element in the character of the runes is illustrated by the fact that the Kylver inscription occurs on a stone buried in a grave as well as by a passage from the early Scandinavian poem *Hávamál*:

> I know that I hung on the windswept tree for nine whole nights pierced by the spear, given to Odin, myself given to myself on that tree whose roots no man knows. They refreshed me neither with bread nor with drink from the horn. I peered down, I learnt runes, howling I learnt them, and then fell back.

There seems, however, no reason to suppose that runes were necessarily magical or religious in origin; it would seem probable that they were primarily and originally used for purposes of normal communication and that they were adapted for religious and magical purposes in an incidental fashion.

The origin of the runes themselves is obscure. They were certainly not a Scandinavian invention and tentative theories would now derive them from the Greek, Roman

10 Silver brooches of the late Roman Iron Age from Swedish graves. The brooches are inlaid with impressed gold sheet and embellished with applied rosettes. The form of the brooch is basically that of the safety-pin and ultimately derives from the European early Iron Age. Top, from Ryet, Strängsered, Västergötland; centre, from Svie, Alva, Gotland, and, bottom, from Havor, Hablingbo, Gotland

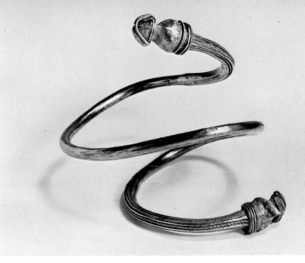

11 Gold arm-ring found in a bog at Vittskövle, Skåne, Sweden. The terminals are formed of stylized snakes' heads and the band itself is decorated with beading along its length. It was probably imported from the south-eastern portion of the Roman Empire (Noricum). Weight: 383·37 grm.

or North Italic-Celtic alphabets, perhaps along the eastern or (less likely) perhaps along the western routes. However we interpret the runes and with whatever origins we endow them, they provide the first evidences of literacy in Scandinavia. From the time of their first appearance the historical record becomes less dark, although it is not until the Viking Age that they add in any marked degree to our knowledge of the Scandinavian people.

Weapons and Dress

From the grave-goods of the Scandinavians in the Roman Iron Age we can see that they were considerably influenced by fashions current in the Roman provinces and in the lands of the Germanic tribes who were clients of the Romans or lived on the borders of the Empire. The shapes and designs of the arm-rings, brooches and gold *Ills 10, 11* pendants worn by the men and women, and the forms of some of the pottery which was used for both cooking and *Ill. 14* storage, were based to some extent on Roman models. Roman ornamental motifs were incorporated into their own art. Occasionally they even attempted to reproduce Roman representational art in their own idiom: provincial Roman statues were copied, drained of naturalism and strengthened by abstract individuality. Roman designs formed the basis for the lively art of the Migration period which is discussed below.

29

12 Stocking-breeches from the great bog-find at Thorsbjerg in Schleswig. Made of wool they have slits at the ankle to allow for ease in dressing. There are loops at the waist for a belt or girdle. The seat of the trousers is formed of a square panel

Their weapons, their clothes and many other aspects of their material culture, however, had nothing to do with the Roman world. The drinking-horns, which have already been mentioned, were not the sort of thing one would expect to see on any self-respecting Roman's table. The weapons – shield, spear and sword – were quite unlike those carried by the regular Roman armies, although the sword, a long-bladed weapon of hard steel, carried in a scabbard which was slung from the belt, was similar in form to that used by the Germanic auxiliaries of the Roman army. The shield was made of thin wooden board with a central iron boss to protect the hand: it was light and was normally circular, although rectangular shields are also known. The spear, with a leaf-shaped blade, and the bow and arrow completed the warrior's armament.

We know little of the dress of the Scandinavians in this period, although a series of finds from the bogs of South Jutland and North Germany give some indication of fashion. The men wore trousers, one pair of which has attached foot-pieces. The trousers were held in place by

Ill. 12

13 Decorated leather belt-end from the bog-find at Vimose. The ornament is derived from a Roman motif. Such belts were decorated with circular bronze mounts which were fastened by means of a lug passing through a slit in the leather

leather belts, some of which may have been decorated. *Ill. 13* The upper part of the body was covered by a jerkin and most men also wore a cloak. Women's clothes of this period have not survived to any great extent; what few clues we have would suggest that they wore a long trailing gown, perhaps made of a single rectangle of cloth fastened at the shoulders by a pair of brooches. To these basic garments would be added hats, shoes and cloaks. Hair was probably elaborately dressed and the men were usually clean-shaven. Most of the surviving dress is of wool, but one must presume that skins and furs were used and traces of linen are also found. The wool appears to have been woven on an upright loom which had a horizontal beam from which the warps were hung and weighted by stones or baked clay rings. The hems of some garments were probably braided in complicated patterns by tablet-weaving.

Although there was a considerable amount of Scandinavian capital tied up in trade, the basic economy of the country was essentially agricultural. The farmer tilled his

14 Pottery of the Roman Iron Age from the grave-field at Valloby, Sjælland, Denmark which produced the Samian ware bowl reproduced in *Ill. 6*. The ware has a black burnished finish

land with an ard – a crooked stick with a point – which was dragged through the ground by an ox or by another human being. The heavier plough, with wheel and mouldboard, is not attested in Scandinavia (according to recent radiocarbon dating) until well after the end of the first millennium of our era. Traces of furrows made by an ard were discovered during excavations at Nørre Fjand in Jutland – appearing as dark stripes running criss-cross over the surface of the fields parallel with their boundaries. Terraced fields divided by banks were also observed; the fields varied in size between about a quarter and three-quarters of an acre. Evidence concerning the crops grown at this period is slight; but from Bornholm we have some indication that barley and oats were grown at different periods of the Roman Iron Age. Harvesting implements of iron are frequently found and the harvested grain was ground on the common saddle-quern which had still not been replaced by the rotary quern. The grain was made into porridge or bread, which was baked either on open fires or in ovens – like the semicircular example found at Dalshøj on the Danish island of Bornholm. Nothing is perhaps so evocative of the everyday life of the ordinary people as a small bread roll from Vikbolandet in Östergötland, Sweden. Sheep, cattle and goats provided meat, dairy produce and clothing for the people, but only the strongest beasts were kept throughout the winter: there would be a large slaughter of all sub-standard animals in the late autumn and their meat, together with fish from the sea, lakes and rivers, would be dried, smoked or salted away against the hard winter months.

Settlements and Houses

The best evidence for houses of the Roman Iron Age comes from excavations in Denmark. Norway and Sweden have also produced a few settlement sites, but the vast area of these two countries makes it impossible to generalize concerning them. In fact, so rarely have settlements of this period been found in Sweden, north of what was for much of its history a Danish province (Skåne), that it is practically impossible to say anything about the form houses took in that country. It is even impossible to say with any certainty whether the common form of settlement in Sweden was the farm or the village, and yet many burial-places, cemeteries and grave-fields are known for which a settlement site has yet to be discovered. Apart from the few houses which have been excavated in Rogaland, evidence for Norwegian settlement sites is sparse.

In Denmark a fair number of farms and villages have been excavated and the evidence suggests that villages were already in existence there at the beginning of our era. Basically the house types follow the form of the earlier houses of the pre-Roman Iron Age and certain generalizations can be made about them. They are rectangular in plan and, save in Fyn where the ridge of the roof was carried on a row of central upright posts, normally had a roof carried on a double row of posts which were presumably tied together in pairs by a cross-beam. The house was either a single chamber or was divided into two by a transverse screen; at one end were the living quarters, a single room with a hearth, and at the other end was a byre. At Ginderup, in North Jutland, the village had been destroyed by fire; in the fire the roof of one of the houses had fallen and the charred remains revealed that it had been supported on rafters between 4 cm. and 8 cm. thick; the rafters themselves having been covered by straw and two layers of turf. The house measured 14·75 m. × 4 m. The east end consisted of a byre with an earth floor, while the living quarters with a clay floor were at the west end. There was a stone-paved entrance in the middle of one of the long sides and underneath it the skeleton of a dog was found – an offering to the gods for the protection of the house. Another house at the same site, which had also been burnt down, had been abandoned with some animals still in the byre – four sheep, a pig and a cow. The buildings at Ginderup varied in detail and, as we examine the different houses on Danish settlement sites of the Roman Iron Age in Jutland, we can see many such variations: at Nørre Fjand the walls were of wattle and daub, or in one case of upright posts, while at Ginderup there is some evidence of turf walls panelled with wood. The remains of a door at Nørre Fjand, 1·25 m. high, perhaps give some indication of the height of the walls of the building.

Ill. 15   All the indoor activities of human life took place in one long, hall-like chamber, usually with a central fire-place. Cooking, sleeping, spinning and quarrelling must have given to these smoky rooms an almost 'gothick' gloom.

15 Reconstructed interior of a farm-house from Tofting, north Germany. Such a house would be typical of many late Roman Iron Age houses in Denmark, with living quarters at one end and byre or storage room at the other

The Sea

The sea was an important element in the life of the Scandinavian peasant; from the sea he drew food, by way of the sea came traders and invaders. We are fortunate in having a fair amount of evidence concerning the ships of the first millennium. All the ships of the pre-Viking era in Scandinavia were propelled by oars and there is no archaeological evidence that sail was used in Scandinavian waters before the Vikings emerged to trouble the world in the late eighth century. The Nydam vessels were found in the last century in a bog in South Jutland and are now in the Schleswig-Holstein Provincial Museum in Schleswig. The largest Nydam vessel is 23·7 m. long and was made *Ill. 16* of oak. Its ribs are formed of natural-grown crooks, to which the planks were tied – clinker fashion – through cleats fashioned out of the solid wood. There is, practically speaking, no keel – merely a thickened plank – and there is no seating for a mast (the smaller boat from Nydam which was built of pine has a slightly more elaborate keel). The rowlocks consist of thorn-shaped pieces of wood lashed to the gunwales and the longish sweeps survive. Boats such as this were large enough to cross the North Sea – after all many an eighteenth-century privateer was no larger – and it may have been in boats like these that the Anglo-Saxons came to England from this very area. Indeed a similar boat, some 26 m. in length, was found at Sutton Hoo in Suffolk, in the grave-like cenotaph of an Anglo-Saxon king who was buried at some date between 625 and 660.

The Kvalsund find from Norway also consists of two ships found in a bog. The largest was 18 m. in length, clinker-built of eight strakes fastened to natural-grown ribs. It has a modest keel and a steering oar on the starboard side. This boat is usually – but tentatively – dated to the seventh century, long after the Roman Iron Age but before the great Viking ships (p. 85) were developed. It has been suggested that the Kvalsund boat may have been rigged for sailing; this is not the place to discuss the possibility of the existence of sailing-ships in Scandinavian waters in the pre-Viking Age, but it should be remembered that Tacitus and other classical authors write convincingly of just such vessels in the southern North Sea at the very beginning of our era – perhaps the archaeological record gives a false picture, based purely on coincidence and accident.

Offerings and the Gods

Both the Kvalsund and Nydam boats were recovered from bogs. The practice of ritual deposition of all sorts of objects is known from many sites in Scandinavia. It is estimated that from the Danish finds from Vimose, Ejsbøl, Kragehul, Nydam, Thorsbjerg and Illerup between fifteen thousand and twenty thousand objects have been re-

16 The ship from Nydam in south Jutland viewed from the stern. The massive steering oar is clearly seen on the starboard side

covered. In Norway and Sweden such deposits are less frequently encountered and are less rich, but the finds from Kvalsund in Norway and from Käringsjön and Skedemosse in Sweden, indicate that the practice was widespread. Besides boats, weapons, treasures of gold and silver, clothing, idols, coins, animals and even human *Ills 17, 18* beings, were placed in these bogs as a sacrifice to the gods. Not only the animals but the weapons themselves were sometimes 'killed' before being placed in the bog: gold and silver objects were bent or rolled up, swords were bent, spears were broken and shields were pierced before being thrown into the bog. Such finds may reflect Julius Caesar's description of the practice of certain German tribes:

They dedicate to Mars [*i.e.* Odin], when they have determined on a decisive battle, such spoil as they may take. When they have conquered, they sacrifice such living things as they have captured and all the other effects they collect into one place. In many states you

17 The ornamented hilts of two-edged iron swords found in a bog at Kragehul, Fyn, Denmark. Dating from the earliest part of the Migration Period these swords were presumably deposited as an offering to the gods after victory

may see piles of these things heaped up on consecrated spots; nor does it often happen that anyone, disregarding the sanctity of the practice, has dared either to hide captured objects in his house, or take away those things set aside; and the severest punishment, with torture, has been ordained for such a deed.

The practice described by Caesar differs in some respects from that encountered in the Scandinavian bog finds, but the fundamental idea may be the same. Although there is a warlike character about many of the finds, they were not assembled and sacrificed at one time but over hundreds of years. At Skedemosse on the Swedish island of Öland, for example, the finds span the period from the third to the sixth century, apart from certain offerings of animals, which have been dated by the radiocarbon method to the period about the birth of Christ. At Skedemosse – as at Ejsbøl – the finds were flung into a lake after the objects had been violently mutilated and often burnt. Human bones of some fifty individuals were also found; they may represent prisoners of war or people chosen specially for sacrifice. Strangely there were no finds of female equipment at Skedemosse – unlike at Thorsbjerg, for example.

It must be emphasized that the offerings have different characteristics at different periods. At Skedemosse we have seen how the earliest finds are largely seasonal offerings of slaughtered animals – representing, presumably, some aspect of prayer for fertility. In the third century the deposition becomes more warlike in character. The fertility aspect of such offerings is demonstrated at Käringsjön in southern Sweden, where wooden farming implements and traces of animal fat, even a bundle of flax, as well as animal bones, were discovered. Such finds can only be seen as reflections of the religion and superstitions of the Scandinavian people; they must be interpreted as thank-offerings, dedicatory offerings or placatory gifts.

18 A section of the offerings found in a peat bog at Illerup, Jutland, Denmark. They include a comb, a number of spearheads and various animal bones. Finds such as these were found scattered over a large area

Until their conversion to Christianity – an object not achieved until the tenth and eleventh centuries – the Scandinavians worshipped a pantheon of gods who have an origin in the common Indo-European tradition. The gods were equated by classical authors with their Roman counterparts – Thor, for example, is similar in many of his aspects to Jupiter. The chief evidence concerning the nature of northern religion comes from medieval Christian sources which were, of course, hostile to such strange gods, but an occasional reference can also be culled from classical texts and poetic sources of the Viking Age. The chief gods were Odin, Thor, Njord and Frey. Odin was the god of poetry, the master of magic; he had great

19, 20 *Above:* Silver amulet in the shape of a Thor's hammer from Bredsätra, Öland, Sweden. It is embellished with filigree ornament which forms a head with the great staring eyes which were one of the attributes of Thor. *Right:* Bronze figure found at Rällinge, Södermanland, Sweden. It represents a sitting man with an erect phallus – perhaps Freyr

power and knowledge, he could hear the grass grow. He was also the god of war and all his followers who fell in battle joined him in Valhalla where they lived a fully heroic life of feasting and fighting. A more popular god – although not so powerful as Odin – was Thor, whose name is associated with thunder: he was immensely strong (his mother was Jörd, which is to be translated as 'Earth'). His symbol – the hammer Mjǫllnir – was very popular as an amulet in Scandinavia and presumably symbolizes his immense physical strength as well as his function as protector of the gods and men. The symbol may well have been used in the consecration of a bride and in association with the burial of the dead. Thor was red-haired, a mighty

Ill. 41

Ill. 20 eater and toper, and rather unsophisticated. Njord was the god of wealth and, like his son Freyr, was associated with fertility. There were other deities, among them Baldr, Tyr, Bragi, and a number of goddesses including Odin's wife Frigg, and Freyja, the goddess of love. The gods lived in Asgard where each had his own hall; here also was Yggdrasil, the sacred tree, beneath which lived the three norns – representing past, present and future – who spin out man's destiny.

Norse mythology is permeated by the principle of evil and leads logically to the destruction of the world (*Ragnarök*) in which it and the gods are consumed by fire and water in the middle of a battle which has raged between the gods and the forces of evil, led by Loki, the instigator of all men's misfortunes. After Ragnarök a new world arises to which the gods return and where happiness, wisdom and fertility come into their own; goodness finally fills everything.

This was not a centrally organized religion; although there were cult places, temples and altars (some of which were more important than others), there was no strict religious discipline. The priests were not set apart, and in isolated regions the temples were probably served by the rich landowners. There was no recognized doctrine, no uniform method of worship; a man chose his own god and went his own way, calling on different gods in different circumstances. In this lack of organization lay the relatively quick collapse of the pagan religion in the face of the Christian Church. It was not difficult to worship the Christian god at the same time; we are told, for example, that a Viking, Helgi the Lean, 'believed in Christ and yet made vows to Thor for sea-voyages or in tight corners, and for everything which struck him as of real importance.' But once Christ was admitted to the pagan pantheon it would not be long before the ancient gods fell to a doctrinally disciplined religious system.

21 Picture-stone from Tjängvide, Gotland, Sweden. The lower field depicts a sailing vessel full of armed warriors. The upper field portrays a building, possibly a representation of Vallhalla, as well as an eight-legged horse (Sleipnir), the rider of which is apparently being greeted by a woman with a drinking horn. Ninth century

It is against this background – a background of warlike gods and gods of fertility – that we must see the Scandinavian votive deposits, and, although they lose their warlike aspect in the sixth century, it is possible to trace in the 'killed' objects found in the graves of the Vikings something of the same religious tradition. The votive deposits and the graves, which contain articles of everyday use intended to accompany the dead person to the

22 Fragment of a memorial slab from Kirk Andreas, Isle of Man. The fragment bears the shaft of a cross filled with interlaced animals. To the left at the bottom is a representation of the legendary hero, Sigurd, slaying the dragon Fafnir. At the top of this field Sigurd is shown roasting the heart of the dragon over a fire, the flames of which are represented by three triangles

future life, provide our chief archaeological evidence for the religion of the North. Archaeological evidence for temples and cult sites has recently been weighed in the balance and found wanting and increased knowledge of these matters awaits further excavation and more critical investigation. Figures of gods are occasionally found.

Ills 19, 20 Thor and Freyr can be identified and Thor's hammer is frequently recognized in the Viking period; it is even possible that figures incised on the memorial stones of *Ill. 21* Gotland represent Baldr, Odin and the other gods while *Ill. 22* certain divine heroes, such as Gunnar and Sigurd, appear frequently in Viking Age carving. These latter representations often occur in Christian contexts, obviously invested with a Christian meaning, and so, although the pagan religion disappeared, the Church retained some of the stories and converted them to their own use.

Chapter Two

The Era of the Great Migrations

Throughout the first millennium, Europe had some of the qualities of a maelstrom: the tribes of Europe were on the move, searching for richer land, fleeing from tyranny, seeking booty or *Lebensraum*. Although Scandinavia was on the edge of this disturbance, it was responsible for some of it. It was from Denmark that the Angles and Jutes moved to conquer and settle in the British Isles; legend would have it that the Goths and Burgundians also had their origin in Scandinavia, but of this there is no evidence. With the collapse of the Roman Empire the movements became almost phrenetic; Huns, Goths, Vandals, wave upon wave of tribes, moved across Europe, giving momentum to the peoples of the Continent. This restless epoch – the Migration period – lasted until the rise of Charlemagne, the crystallization of the main European states, and the coming of the Vikings in the late eighth century.

There are few historical sources for Scandinavia in the Migration period, all that survive are incidental references in Mediterranean, Frankish and Anglo-Saxon sources, often little more than a reference to a tribe or its chief. Certain episodes in Scandinavian history are hinted at, but no consecutive story is revealed; only a rather shadowy impression of an area racked by internecine war – as the Svíar of Uppland, for instance, attempted to gain control of Sweden, as the Danes fought the Norwegians, as Frisia was raided by Swedes. Once again archaeology is the key to an understanding of the period where historical sources are slender, contradictory and almost legend.

23 Rings and bars of gold from the largest surviving Swedish gold treasure of the Migration Period. It was found in 1904 at Timboholm, Skövde, in Västergötland, and weighs a little more than seven kilograms. It is here reproduced at about one-third of its natural size

In the greater part of Scandinavia this was a wealthy period, and, although times were troubled, the people of the northern countries appear to have increased in political and economic stature, perhaps because of the comparative stability of their economy and the absence of serious threat from outside their borders. Although never free from internal trouble – as many a violently destroyed farm dramatically relates in the archaeological record – the Scandinavians were building up a self-confident civilization of their own between 400 and 800, which was largely independent of outside influence and which reached its full-blooded maturity with the Viking adventure. The seeds of this adventure were sown in these four hundred years and the harvest was gathered in between 800 and 1100. In Sweden the Migration period and the period of two hundred years before the Viking adventure began (the Vendel period) has been described as an age of gold.

Some of the plunder of Europe seems to have rubbed off on their fingers: a gold hoard found at Tureholm in Södermanland in 1774 weighed some 12 kilos, and another from Timboholm in Västergötland weighed 7 kilos.

Ill. 23

Scandinavia was rich, and in no place is this better seen than in the graves of the wealthy families of Sweden. Considerable mounds were erected over the dead and bodies were sometimes placed in a ship which was then covered by an earthen mound. In certain cases, mostly in the early Viking Age, the burial was surrounded by a setting of stones in the form of a ship, with taller stones at each end to represent the rising prow and stern-posts of a real vessel. The association of the ship with death has deep roots (in Scandinavia there is evidence of some such belief as early as the Bronze Age); the idea of a voyage on the uncharted seas of death is natural to any seafaring man, and we may perhaps peep into the mind of the period through the words of an Anglo-Saxon poet who was describing a Scandinavian chieftain's funeral. Although in this description from the epic poem *Beowulf* the ship is not buried in a mound, the idea which lies behind it would be familiar to the Scandinavian of the Migration, Vendel or Viking period who buried his chieftain with great state:

Ill. 24

There at the quay, stood a ring-prowed ship –
The radiant and eager ship of the lord.
They laid down the beloved lord,
The giver of rings, in the bosom of the ship,
The lord lay by the mast. They brought from afar
Many great treasures and costly trappings.
I never heard of a ship so richly furnished as this,
With weapons of war, armour of battle,
Swords and corslets. Many treasures lay
Piled on his breast.

24 Stone ship-setting from Vätteryd, Norra Mellby, Skåne, Sweden, photographed during the excavations of 1955. 257 m. long it is built of up-ended stones. There was no central grave but there were remains of a number of pits containing burnt bone as well as five hearths. This is but one grave from one of the largest cemeteries of the later Iron Age in Skåne.

Such ships were uncovered during the excavation of two great cemeteries in Uppland – at Vendel and Valsgärde – but other ship burials of almost equal wealth have also been recorded from other parts of Scandinavia, from Lackalänge in Skåne for example. The graves of the fifth and sixth centuries had been plundered at Valsgärde – a feature noted elsewhere in Sweden – and only seventh- and eighth-century graves survive. An idea of the impressive nature of the earlier graves can be gained from the royal cemetery at Old Uppsala, a short distance from the *Ill. 25* modern town of Uppsala. The four largest mounds form part of a large cemetery and are set in line on a ridge. The westernmost is the largest, some 12 m. high, and is only surpassed in height by one other Swedish mound, *Anund's* mound in Badelunda, Västmanland, although the great Norwegian mound in Romerike, known as Raknehaugen, is 95 m. in diameter and 19 m. high. The finds from the three excavated Uppsala mounds are disappointing, but they do enable us to confirm the dating of these graves to the Migration period and to identify the dynasty and even possibly the kings who were buried here. From both Norse and Anglo-Saxon sources we have evidence of a royal family known as the Ynglingr; one king, Egil, is said in these sources to have been buried beneath a mound at Uppsala. Intelligent guess-work would suggest that

25 The grave-mounds at Old Uppsala, Sweden. At least one king of the royal dynasty of Uppland – the Ynglingr – is said to have been buried here, but prolonged excavations at this most famous of all Swedish sites have produced few objects of the type one might expect in a royal cemetery. The church in the background is traditionally the site of the pagan temple described by Adam of Bremen

26 Helmet from grave XIV at Vendel, Uppland, Sweden. The cheek and neck-guards are of iron.
The cap is also of iron, but is covered by impressed bronze sheets which portray a procession of
warriors around the brow and fighting men above the eye-brows. The cap is crossed by bands of
bronze plates impressed with interlace patterns

27 Helmet from grave I at Vendel, Uppland, Sweden. Constructed like the helmet figured *opposite*, its applied plates bear scenes of a rider and of a bear. A helmet of similar form, almost certainly made in Sweden, was found in the cenotaph of a seventh-century East Anglian king at Sutton Hoo, in Suffolk. Also found in this English grave were other Swedish arms

three of the princes buried beneath these great mounds were Aun, Egil and Adils, all of whom appear in *Ynglinga-saga*. A fourth prince, Ottar, was perhaps buried a few miles away in a mound already known by his name at the end of the seventeenth century. Old Uppsala was also an important cult centre and the site of a temple, details of which are recorded by Adam of Bremen.

The aristocratic Swedish cemeteries at Vendel and Valsgärde have yielded a series of rich burials which extend from the Migration period into the Viking period. As we have seen, many of the dead were buried in boats and with them were found richly ornamented swords, *Ills 26, 27* elaborate helmets, bridle mounts, shields embellished with highly ornamented bosses and charges, brooches, glass and more everyday objects such as tools, combs and vessels. Not only were inanimate objects laid in the graves, but the boats and their occupants were some-times accompanied by horses – often more than one – which were placed alongside, in the trench built to receive the ship. The burials at Vendel and Valsgärde can only be considered as the burials of chieftains, for no other class of society could have borne the capital expenditure in-volved in the sacrifice of these costly treasures. The lavishness of the burials gives a remarkable impression not only of the wealth of the family, but also of the solidly based economy of middle Sweden.

Grave-finds of similar richness have not yet been found in either Denmark or Norway, but some cemeteries in these countries reflect an only slightly less wealthy society. Lousgård, on the Danish island of Bornholm, provided a burial-place for a rich aristocratic family, at least one member of which was accompanied to the grave by a sacrificed slave. The five graves at Snartemo, Vest Agder, provide a Norwegian parallel. Here again can be seen abundant wealth: rich weapons, glass vessels, bronze bowls, gold rings as well as humbler objects.

28 Detail of the Migration Period gold neck-rings from Trolleberg, Flackarp and Ryd, Skabersjö, Skane, Sweden. Their weight is a symbol of the wealth of this period, the first weighs almost a kilogram and the second (the outer one) weighs about one and a quarter kilograms

Wealth and Trade, Loot and War

The great hoards which were mentioned at the beginning of this chapter are symptomatic of a period of trouble and war. Hoards tend to be buried in time of danger, and the fact that they are found today and were never reclaimed indicates that the fear of the original owner was not misplaced. The hoards chiefly belong to the fifth and early sixth centuries and represent bullion – the portable wealth of a family or person. Many of the objects they contain are unornamented rings and spirals made of plain gold *Ill. 23* bands, and such things may well have been made to some sort of standard of weight; other objects have great beauty and are extremely skilfully made. The great neck- *Ills 28, 29* rings of Sweden, for example, are amongst the most perfect pieces of European jewellery of the period. One hoard symbolizes the wealth of this period and provides one of the most romantic and popular stories of Danish archaeology. The two golden horns from Gallehus were *Ill. 31* made at the period of transition from the Roman Iron Age to the Migration period. The first was found in 1639 and the second in 1734 in the same field at Tønder, South Jutland. They were stolen from the Royal Collection in Copenhagen in 1802 and melted down by the thief before he was caught. We know them now only through contemporary drawings and a reconstruction made soon after their loss. The saddest aspect of this story is that copies

29 Gold collar from Färjestaden, Öland, Sweden. Each band is decorated with filigree wire; small impressed gold plates in the form of circlets, birds or animals, fill the spaces between each ring

were made for presentation before the theft, but none of them can now be traced, one copy indeed was lost at sea off Corsica on its way to join the collection of Cardinal Stephen Borgia. The horns consisted of a plain inner shell and an outer shell made up of several cylinders; one was 2 ft 9 in. long, the other 1 ft 9 in. One bore a runic inscription which may be translated: 'I Hlégestr of Holt [?] made the horn.' They were decorated with applied and engraved figures, which presumably had mythological significance, as well as animal ornament of a type which we will consider below.

30 Hilt and upper part of a rich sixth-century sword from grave V at Snartemo, Hägebostad, ▷ Vest Agder, Norway. The grip is covered with gold plate and the other mounts are silver-gilt. The mount at the mouth of the scabbard and the gold plates bear decoration in Style I animal ornament

The gold coins – *solidi* from the Mediterranean – found
so frequently in the hoards indicate the ultimate source of
the metal and perhaps even of the wealth of these people.
The trade which had grown during the Roman Iron Age
continued through the succeeding periods and, as quality
luxury goods became rarer in southern Europe and as the
Scandinavians developed a refined and distinctive taste of
their own, gold became one of the most desirable of all
imports. Despite the occasional occurrence of luxury
goods, such as glass, in the graves, it is perhaps significant
that a common find in the richer graves – as at Snartemo

Ill. 32 – is a pair of scales, sometimes with weights, which were
presumably used for weighing precious metals in the
course of mercantile transactions. The natural wealth of
the North continued to provide a surplus for export.

It is during this period that we find the first settlement
which can properly be called a trading post. It is hardly
a town; but Helgö, an island in Lake Mälar not very far
from Stockholm in the centre of what was once a kingdom of the Svíar, is the first settlement in Scandinavia

31 Impressions of the two horns which were destroyed in 1802 from Gallehus, Tønder, Jutland, Denmark. The figures were probably applied separately to the horns and the inscription and the background ornament were engraved

32 Pair of bronze scales from a Viking Age grave at Jåtten, Hetland Rogaland, Norway, found together with eight lead weights in a small linen bag. Scales of this type are found throughout the post-Roman Iron Age and must have been part of the standard equipment of any trader

that can be recognized as not having had a primarily agricultural or military basis. Excavation since 1954 has revealed a series of houses set either on terraces on the rocky slopes above the shore or on the flatter low-lying shore itself. Apparently founded in the fifth century, it began to lose its importance in the late eighth century, when the near-by town of Birka began to dominate the area. Excavation has not yet revealed the full extent of the site nor all the implications of its enormous importance, but the results so far reveal an economic unit of considerable significance. Imported goods of glass, metal- *Ill. 35* work and pottery reveal connections with western Europe and the Mediterranean, as well as with Poland, Finland and the Baltic states. Perhaps the most incredible object *Ill. 33* symbolizing such connections is the sixth- or seventh-century bronze figure of a Buddha which, presumably through many intermediate hands, reached Sweden from the valleys of northern India, from Kashmir or Afghanistan. Helgö was also a centre of industry, producing among other things a vast quantity of cheap jewellery

33 Bronze figure of Buddha from northern India brought in the Migration Period to the trading station on the small island of Helgö in Lake Mälar, in central Sweden. On the forehead is a gold cast mark. The eyes are inlaid with silver

34 Detail of a hoard from Dalshøj, Bornholm. There were seventeen late Roman gold coins, four gold fragments and a silver-gilt brooch in the hoard, which was probably laid down just before the near-by village was destroyed by fire

35 Detail of the head of a small enamelled bronze crozier from Helgö, the trading station from which the small Buddha figured *opposite* came. It came from the British Isles, perhaps from Ireland and may well have come to Sweden as Viking loot. It dates from the eighth century

cast in bronze from clay moulds found in great abundance in one area of the site; there is, moreover, evidence of ironworking and various other crafts.

But the times were troubled. At Sorte Muld and Dalshøj in Bornholm, for example, farms were burnt down and, as a grim reminder of the fate of the people who were buried there, hoards are found in the vicinity of the buildings. The inhabitants had not been protected by a near-by encampment which they had built in the neighbourhood against just such an eventuality. This attack in the early sixth century came at much the same time as similar troubles in the Swedish offshore island of Gotland. Professor Stenberger has demonstrated, by a study of the coins found in them, that the deposition of hoards in the Baltic islands took place during relatively short periods. The hoards on Öland were probably laid down between 480 and 490, while on Gotland they were deposited between 500 and 520. On both islands traces are found of destroyed settlements at about this time.

Ill. 34

This was, therefore, a period when defence was an important element in the lives of the Scandinavians of the Baltic, and large numbers of forts or strongholds were built in areas which were easily accessible to raiders from

36, 37 *Left:* The fortified encampment at Ismantorp, Långlöt, Öland, is about 125 m. in diameter and has nine gates in its massive wall which still stands to a height of 4 m. Excavations have not produced much dating evidence, but it is generally held that the camp was built at the end of the Roman Iron Age or in the early Migration Period. *Right:* The fortified village of Eketorp, Gräsgård, Öland, is obviously closely related to Ismantorp in plan. This view was taken at the end of the 1968 excavation season. The line of the outer palisade can be seen outside the main bank, the houses of which can be seen within the walls belonging to the earliest phase of settlement – the fifth century

the sea. Many of these forts must have been built during the Migration period as temporary refuges to which people fled in time of sudden invasion by pirates or politically inspired raiders. They were usually set on eminences, sometimes far from the coast, sometimes far from arable land, and in time of trouble a man would retreat to them with his family, his livestock and his portable treasure. The island of Öland provides the most dramatic example of such a refuge: among some rather modest enclosures are two fantastic circular fortifications, which were used over a very long period. These sites – Gråborg and *Ill. 36* Ismantorp – are set in the barren central limestone region

of this island, far from the coast and from arable land. The largest is Gråborg which is about 200 m. in diameter and was used intermittently over a period of a thousand years, being refortified in the late Middle Ages. Throughout the island the ruins of abandoned farms of this period demonstrate the need for these forts.

In at least one place a community tried to fortify itself permanently from such inroads. Professor Mårten Stenberger has, since 1964, been excavating a fortified site *Ill. 37* – Eketorp – on the edge of the barren limestone region of central Öland almost at the southern tip of the island. The fort is circular, 80 m. in diameter, and surrounded by a bank of stone, which may originally have been about 6 m. high; 10 m. from the wall a timbered palisade gave additional protection to the stronghold. The place was inhabited between about 450 and 700/750 and again between the beginning of the eleventh and the end of the thirteenth century; it was probably deserted between these two periods. Finds indicate that Eketorp was a permanent settlement whose occupants pursued the normal economic course of an agricultural community, cultivating the fields round the edge of the near-by lake and raising stock, brewing beer and supporting certain local craftsmen, such as a smith. A few imported objects – particularly glass – suggest a reasonably good economy as does a small hoard of gold. Eketorp, however, is an important – if, as far as we know at present, atypical – phenomenon in the northern countries, as it is the first known permanently inhabited Scandinavian fortification. It provides evidence of a close-knit community, living in houses with party walls set radially around the edge of the circle formed by the defending bank of the settlement. There were probably about forty such buildings round this circle; not all were dwelling-houses (some were byres and store-houses), but they were all constructed in the same fashion: they had foundations of stone, and these were probably crowned by turf walls and roofed with turf supported by a row of central posts. The plan of the Ismantorp fort is similar, but trial excavations have shown this to be empty of settlement material. This led to the previously held belief that these forts were temporary refuges; now that Eketorp has belied this, perhaps we shall have to reconsider the function of other sites.

New Land and Homeland

A cause and a consequence of the newly found riches of the Scandinavian people was the settlement of new territory on the basis of a new economy, an economy designed

38 Remains of a house at Vallhagar, Fröjel, Gotland. This is the largest Migration Period settlement site so far excavated in Scandinavia and the house shown here is typical of the twenty-four that were uncovered between 1946 and 1950. Finds showed that the settlement was inhabited between the early Roman Iron Age and the end of the Migration Period. The photograph clearly shows the entrance at each gable end and the post-holes for the timbers which helped to support the roof

to produce goods for trade to the south. In search of furs, iron, horn and ivory the Norwegians and Swedes turned to the North. In the greater part of northern Scandinavia there had lived since the Stone Age a people whose economy was based on hunting, and fishing, where·the chief tools were made of bone and stone and where iron and bronze was a luxury. In the northern provinces of Norway and Sweden, from the beginning of the Vendel period, we begin to find graves and casual types of evidence which demonstrate a movement by the Swedes towards the Norwegian border along the river valleys leading to the rich north-west coast of Norway. At the

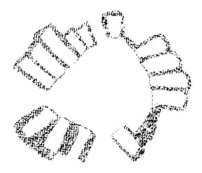

39 Sketch plan of a complex of houses set round a central courtyard at Lekskaren, Rogaland, in the south-west of Norway. The gable ends were either open or built of timber. They are an odd feature of two specific areas, having no apparent economic function

same time the search for wealth caused the settlement of many of the non-arable districts of Norway by expansion along the coast and into the fjords and mountains: settlement sites indicate an interest in stock-breeding, hunting and iron extraction. That these specialist industries were successful is obvious from the rich character of the graves of the area.

In the original homelands there is much evidence of settlement and houses. The destruction of many settlements in the Baltic islands provides a unique opportunity to study the houses of the period between 400 and 600. The foundations of some 2,300 large rectangular houses of this period have been discovered on the islands of Öland and Gotland alone. They vary in length between 5 m. and 60 m. and are usually grouped together as three or four structures loosely related to other houses in similar groups. Such groups are surrounded by a farmyard of which the crumbling walls often survive.

Vallhagar on Gotland is the best known of these settlements. Excavation has revealed some five or six farms comprising some twenty-four buildings and three gravefields. *Ill. 38* The Vallhagar houses are typical of all the Gotland buildings of this period. Each house had limestone wall foundations, and the roof, which may have been of turf or reeds, was supported on a double row of posts. Entrances were usually placed at the gable-ends and there was a hearth on the main axis. In two cases the houses were like those recorded in the Roman Iron Age in Denmark, where the living quarters were at one end and a byre was screened off at the other end. Among the finds analysed was grain; oats were not found, but barley was recovered and wheat and rye also occurred. Sheep and cattle bones were found in a proportion of about 2:1, pig as well as horses were also kept.

Excavations at Vorbasse in Denmark have uncovered *Ill. 87* seven eighth-century farms set along a village street. Each farm-yard includes a main house, wells and other ancilliary buildings (including sunken-floored huts). This is the most perfect example of such a nucleated settlement in Denmark. A strange form of Norwegian barrack-like settlement is typified at Lekskaren, Rogaland, and is found only *Ill. 39* in this area (round Stavanger) and in northern Norway. Such settlements consist of a series of long houses ranged so that their gable-ends face an open central space. The lack of definite byre-like buildings and associated field complexes might suggest that they were refuges like the forts of Öland.

Art and Design

During this period of wealth and expansion the peoples of Scandinavia were becoming conscious of their own taste. One of the most remarkable expressions of this self-confidence is seen in their art, for it was during the last stages of the Roman Iron Age and the beginning of the Migration period that there developed in Scandinavia the beginnings of an art which in one of its aspects at least – animal ornament – was to continue in an unbroken tradition until the end of the Viking Age. Two separate forms of ornament spanned this period: a naturalistic art *Ill. 40* of surprising quality and sensitivity and an abstract art of striking originality and extreme tortuousness. It is hard

40 Animal scratched on the back of a sixth-century square-headed brooch from Nordheim, Hedrum, Vestfold, Norway. One of the rare occurrences of naturalism in the art of this period – typically it is found casually placed on an otherwise formally decorated object

to evaluate the naturalistic art as so little of it survives, but where it is encountered its assured quality demonstrates that this was a rich vein in the art of the North and *Ills 41–46* one would wish to see more of it. Instead we are presented with an intimate and sophisticated abstract art, individual but brilliant and not to everyone's taste; it is an applied art, appearing almost exclusively as an embellishment on objects of daily use. It is seen on brooches and swords, on pendants and helmets, it appears on metal and it appears on stone. Wood must also have been used, but, although this would be the natural medium for the Scandinavian

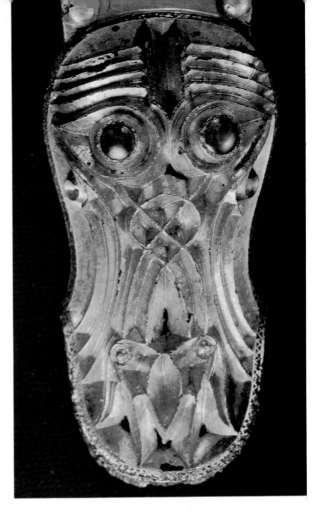

41 Roman medallions were imitated by the Scandinavians between the sixth and eighth centuries in the form of impressed gold sheets adapted as pendants and known as *bracteates*. The Roman origin can easily be seen in the centres of the three upper examples, the main design of which is based on the bust of the Roman emperor. Others bear designs based on what are presumed to be mythological scenes, while others are decorated with animal ornament of normal Migration Period type

42 Gilt-bronze animal mask from a strap-end found in a seventh-century grave at the rich Swedish cemetery at Vendel, Uppland. The eyes of the mask are of garnets, each of which also forms the centre of the hip of an animal executed in Style II. The heads can be seen at the bottom of the mount. The elongated foot forms a frond-like element at one side of the field. The Style II animal in *Ill. 46* came from a mount in the same grave

artist, no major piece of decorative art can be seen in this medium until the beginning of the Viking Age. The art is remarkable, its elements tease our vision and often degenerate into patterns the meaning of which can only be recognized by the trained eye. It is related to the art of northern Europe, to the art of all the Germanic people and was apparently impervious to the more formal ornament of the Mediterranean with its emphasis on naturalism.

The main element of this abstract art is a semi-naturalistic animal ornament which has its roots in the

44–46 *Left*, Detail of the fragmentary square-headed brooch from Langlo, Stokke, Vestfold, Norway, showing a reasonably logical example of Style I animal. *Centre*, the treatment of human figure as seen on the face of the Snartemo sword not seen in *Ill. 30*. The body is split up into its component parts and is already beginning to lose some of its logicality. *Right*, an animal on a belt-mount from grave XII at Vendel, Uppland, Sweden. The animal, of classic Style II type, shows the sinuous characteristics and articulated nature of the newly introduced art of the seventh century

43 Square-headed brooch from Nordheim, Hedrum, Vestfold, Norway. Of late fifth-century date, this brooch exhibits some of the earliest elements of Style I animal ornament. The highly carved surface of the object is typical of the chip-carving which was used by Germanic craftsmen throughout western Europe in the execution of this early animal style. Brooches of a very closely related form are found in Anglo-Saxon graves in England

late Roman Iron Age, when animal designs based on Romano-Germanic originals occur on objects made in Scandinavia. These objects are mostly made of impressed *Ills 42, 43* metal, but the introduction of a new technique, derived from the provincial Roman repertoire, changed these semi-naturalistic creatures into much more elaborate forms. This technique was chip-carving, a method of cutting a flat surface with the corner of a chisel into a series of facets so that the objects would glitter in any light; it was adapted from woodworking to jewellery and appears in silver and bronze, metals which were often *Ills 44, 45* gilded or inlaid with niello – the black sulphide of silver.

More than sixty years ago a Swedish archaeologist, Bernhard Salin, divided the art of the period from 400 to 900 into Styles I, II and III. Although this system has been modified by the recognition of many sub-styles, it still holds good in the main and can appropriately be used here. The art of Style I is based on a contorted, multi-

faceted single animal. Between the time when this animal appears, towards the end of the fifth century, and the period when it is replaced by the Style II animal, a hundred or so years later, it becomes more distorted and degenerate until it reaches a stage where it is almost unrecognizable.

An interesting sidelight is thrown on the origin of this style if we examine the series of impressed gold circular *Ill. 41* pendants, known as bracteates, which are found in some quantity in Scandinavia. These pendants bear a design which is based on the profile portrait of a Roman emperor of the type found on coins and medallions. This motif is subsequently adapted and changed until the head becomes grotesque. Ultimately the bust disappears completely and is replaced by Style I ornament. We can see here, I believe, an expression of the Scandinavian abhorrence of the naturalistic in its applied art.

At the end of the sixth century Style II was introduced *Ill. 46* in Scandinavia from southern Europe and captured the imagination of the inhabitants, who became fascinated by it and raised it to the heights of its expression in the rich graves of Vendel and Valsgärde. Style II is based on interlaced animals of ribbon-like form and the slow curves of this style, executed in chip-carved gilt bronze, appeared in a variety of forms to delight the eye of the Scandinavian until the end of the eighth century, when it was absorbed and changed into the more fussy art of the Viking period. It was this style which, towards the beginning of the Viking era, fined into the rather more complicated Style III, the first truly Viking style.

Chapter Three

The Viking Attack

In a word, although there were an hundred hard-steeled iron heads on one neck, and an hundred sharp, ready, cool, never rusting, brazen tongues in each head, and an hundred garrulous, loud, unceasing voices from each tongue, they could not recount or narrate, enumerate or tell, what all the Irish suffered in common, both men and women, laity and clergy, old and young, noble and ignoble, of hardships and of injuring and of oppression, in every house, from those valiant, wrathful, purely pagan people.

This hyperbolic passage from an Irish writer of the twelfth century summarizes the impression which the Vikings made on the western European mind. Wild statements of this sort have coloured all discussion of the great Viking adventure which brought Scandinavia for the first time into political contact with the rest of the known world. The story which is to be told in this chapter concerns the gradual rise of an empire which, at the beginning of the eleventh century, stretched in theory from North Cape to the Isles of Scilly and admitted a Scandinavian king as an equal to his brothers in the rest of Christendom. It is the story of voyages of exploration, to Iceland, Greenland and America, of merchant journeys into the heart of Asia and of theft and rapine in the Western Isles.

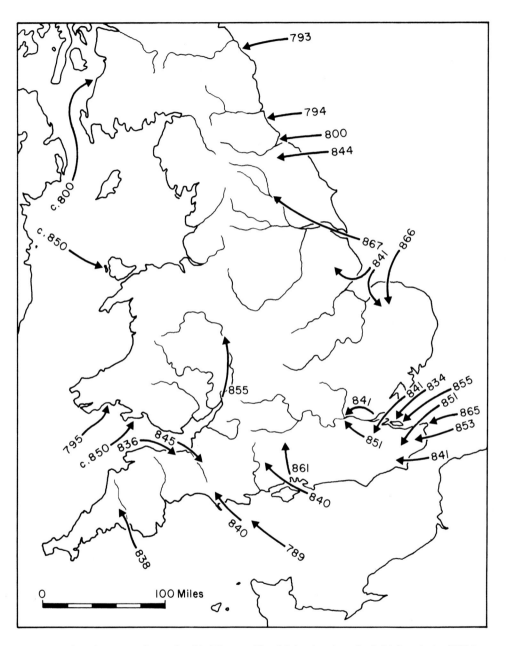

47 Map, based on one drawn by Sir Thomas Kendrick, showing the initial period of Viking attacks on England, starting in 789 and leading up to the capture of York in 867

In Britain and Western Europe

In Western Europe the Viking activities are well documented, and if the clerical chroniclers tend to become rather hysterical about the Viking progress they apparently had some reason. An initial adventure of the Vikings *Ill. 47* on the south coast in 789 encompassed the murder of the King's official representative in the area. This was followed in 793 by the sack of Lindisfarne, the monastery of St Cuthbert. The English scholar Alcuin wrote from the court of Charlemagne expressing his surprise and that of the Western world at such an attack:

> . . . never before has such terror appeared in Britain as we have now suffered from a pagan race, nor was it thought that such an inroad from the sea could be made. Behold, the church of St Cuthbert spattered with the blood of the priests of God, despoiled of all its ornaments; a place more venerable than all in Britain is given as prey to pagan peoples.

From 835 onwards hardly a year passes in which there is no reference in the pages of the *Anglo-Saxon Chronicle* to Viking attacks on England. In 851 they spent their first winter in England, in 865 they took the Danegeld (a vast political bribe) for the first time, while in 867 the character of the raids changed when Healfdene seized York and finally settled in 876 in the old English kingdom of Northumbria. Finally in 886 the treaty of Alfred with Guthrum gave to the Scandinavians the right to settle in the north of England and in the Five Boroughs – Nottingham, Lincoln, Stamford, Derby and Leicester. The Vikings ruled these areas in their own right and incursions from Dublin and Norway added the northwest of England to their area of influence in the early tenth century. By the middle of the tenth century, however, all these areas were nominally back under English control and it was not until early in the next century that

Scandinavian kings reigned again in England. The eleventh-century Viking conquest was of a different type, a conquest carried out for political aggrandizement and an increase of royal revenue.

These incursions have left traces in the archaeological record. Coin hoards and a handful of pagan-style burials tell of the troubled state of England up to the time of Healfdene's settlement and Alfred's treaty, while Christian memorials in the Scandinavian taste and Viking elements in the art tell of the reconciliation of two cultures. More striking perhaps is the evidence of the place-names. In the East Riding of Yorkshire for example, 40 per cent

Ill. 48

48 On this cross from Middleton, Yorkshire, carved in the last quarter of the ninth century, can be seen a Viking warrior laid out in his grave with his weapons – shield, helmet, sword, knife and spear. This mixture of paganism and Christianity is typical of the initial period of settlement of England when the Christian religion was just beginning to make itself felt on a loosely pagan people

of the place-names recorded in Domesday Book are of Scandinavian origin; in the North Riding, 38 per cent; in the West Riding only between 13 and 19 per cent. Even the names of some towns were changed; *Northworthig* became Derby, *Streoneshalh* became Whitby. But many villages and towns retained their old names, although the Viking presence is attested by graves or memorials in the Viking taste. Although the point is disputed it seems on this evidence that there was a considerable population incursion into England in the ninth century. The raids and subsequent events can also be recognized in Scandinavia. In many of the Viking graves of Norway, for example, are fragments of Anglo-Saxon metalwork, adapted as ornaments by the men and women of the North – some, at least, rudely torn from their original settings on books and shrines. In Sweden more than thirty thousand Anglo-Saxon coins in the great hoards of the tenth and eleventh centuries reflect the Danegeld – the tax paid by the English to their conquerors, a tax which is sometimes recorded on runic memorial stones to Viking warriors, as at Yttergärde in Uppland, Sweden, where a stone was erected by Karse and Karlbjörn in memory of their father Ulv of Borresta: 'And Ulv has taken three gelds in England. That was the first that Tosti paid, then Thorkel paid, then Cnut paid.' The rune-stones tell us more of these attacks, personalizing the attackers in the time of Cnut, as for example on the Nävelsjö stone from the Swedish province of Småland: 'Gunnkel set this stone in memory of Gunnar his father, Rode's son. Helgi laid him in a stone coffin in England in Bath.'

England was not the only western European country to receive attention from the Vikings. The Faroe Isles, northern Scotland, the Scottish Isles, the Isle of Man and Ireland were all settled by the Vikings. Viking kings and chiefs proliferated and founded such towns as Dublin, Cork and Limerick to further their trade and act as bases

Ill. 51

Ills 52, 53

49–51 *Above*, slab from Otley, Yorkshire, decorated in the eleventh-century Ringerike style. The same style being also clearly seen on the slab, *below*, which was found in the churchyard of St Paul's Cathedral in London. These two stones reflect the Viking taste which made itself felt in England during the reign of Cnut. The same style is seen, *right*, on the stone from Yttergärde, Orkesta, Uppland, Sweden which tells of a man, Ulv, who made three expeditions to England in the early eleventh century

for piratical attacks which they mounted on both England and the Continent (the north-west of England was largely settled by Norwegians based on Dublin and Man). The Low Countries and France did not escape the Viking incursions; between 841 and 844 Quentovic, Rouen and Nantes were attacked and ruthlessly sacked. The great port of Dorestad at the mouth of the Rhine was for some time controlled by a Viking, Rorik, who was virtually the ruler of the Low Countries. Paris and Trier were attacked and in 911 the Norwegians settled Normandy. Spain was

52 In the bottom corner of an early churchyard at Balladoole, Arbory, Isle of Man, a Viking warrior was buried in his ship. The outline of the grave is clearly seen in this aerial photograph, slighting the wall of the graveyard. The grave also cuts through a number of pre-Viking Christian burials. The Vikings in Man and elsewhere – even in the earliest periods of settlement – often used existing Christian cemeteries for the burial of their dead

53 Oval brooch from a late ninth-century grave in the large Viking cemetery at Pierowall, Westray, in the rich Viking earldom of Orkney.

raided in the mid ninth century; indeed the whole of the western seaboard of Europe and towns on many of the major river entries into the Continent received the attention of Vikings in search of plunder and booty.

The New Lands in the Ocean

Possibly the greatest adventures of the Vikings in the West were in the Atlantic, where they discovered new lands – Iceland, Greenland and North America. According to Ari the Wise, writing about 1130, Iceland was inhabited by Irish monks before the Vikings arrived in the late ninth century. No archaeological trace of these inhabitants has yet been discovered, but it seems likely that Iceland was known to the Vikings before the traditional date of 860 for the first three Viking voyages of exploration by a Swede, Gardar Svavarson, and two Norwegians, Naddod and Flokki Vilgerdason. The land-hungry Vikings liked what they saw; indeed one of Flokki's party reported that every blade of grass dripped with butter – a judgement which is difficult to understand when one considers the colours of this bleak and practically treeless country. About ten years later the settlement of Iceland began. Ari, in his history, the *Íslendingabók*, tells of this settlement:

Iceland was first settled from Norway in the days of Harald Fairhair, son of Halfdan the Black according to the opinion and calculation of Teit my foster-father . . . and of my paternal uncle Thorkel Gellisson who remembered far back, and of Thurid daughter of Snorri the *goði* who was both learned in many things and trustworthy . . . 870 years after the birth of Christ.

A Norwegian called Ingólf, it is reliably reported, first went thence to Iceland when Harald Fairhair was sixteen winters old, and for the second time a few winters later. He settled south in Reykjarvík. It is called Ingólfshöfði [Ingólf's Head], east of Minþakseyri, where he made his first landing, and Ingólfsfell, west of Ölfossá, where he took possession of land.

In the course of the next fifty or sixty years all the suitable land had been taken. *Landnámabók* gives the names of about four hundred of the chief settlers, but many more people must have come into the country – thirty-five of these settlers, for instance, came, it is explicitly stated, in their own ships. It has been calculated that by the middle of the tenth century between three thousand and four thousand families, representing perhaps some fifty thousand to sixty thousand people, were living in the country. On the basis of the literary sources we can say that about half of them came from the area round the present-day town of Bergen in Norway – the area of the *Gulatingslag* – and were apparently fleeing from the tyranny of Harald Fairhair who was trying to establish his authority in western Norway. Others came from other parts of Scandinavia and many from the Viking areas of Britain. In Iceland was established a republic of semi-aristocratic character, at first ruled over by the secular priests (*goði*), thirty-two of whom became in 930 the first members of the consultative assembly – the Althing – with one of their number Úlfljót as *Lögsögumaðr* (law

54 The great cleft in the rock at Thingvellir, immediately above the meeting-place of the Icelandic national assembly. This was the scene of many of the most important events in Icelandic history, including that which took place in 1000, when the law-speaker, Thorgeir proclaimed that all men in Iceland should be baptized and become Christian

speaker or chairman). The Althing (backed by a series of local assemblies) met each summer at Thingvellir not far *Ill. 54* from Reykjavík and fulfilled many purposes; as a court for promulgating the law, as a fair and as a social occasion. Over the years its character changed and its numbers grew until the Norwegian king, Håkon Håkonsson, took control of Iceland in 1262–4. In this rich country with its teeming rivers, flocks of tender sea-birds, good pasture, its seals and whales, a strong society grew up whose doings are recorded in sagas and other tales which have their roots in the tenth and eleventh centuries, but were not written down until the thirteenth century. These stories are great literature; the best – the sagas of Njal, Egil and the Laxdalers, for example – are exciting and fascinating reading to this day; they and the splendid poetry of the late tenth century open a window into the history of Iceland and, more important, into the minds of the people who settled this vast land a thousand years ago. The sagas need careful sifting if we are to draw history from them, but it is through them that Iceland's claim to have contributed to the European cultural heritage is most successfully made.

From Iceland to Greenland, across the Denmark Strait, is no great distance, and it was not long before the settlers of Iceland discovered this forbidding and gloomy land with its inhospitable coastline penetrated on the western side of the country by deep fjords. The man who is credited with the settlement of Greenland was called Erik the Red, and he came from Jaeder in Norway, having had to leave in a hurry, 'because of some killings.' He got into trouble in Iceland and, about 980, was outlawed. He determined to go in search of a land which a storm-tossed Icelander called Gunnbjörn Ulf-Krakason had seen, but not landed on, some fifty years earlier. Erik rounded Cape Farewell and spent three years in exploring the land between Herjolfsnes (Ikigait) and Eiriksfjord (Tunugd-liarfik). He named the country Greenland and, having sailed back to Iceland, where he ran into more trouble, he decided to settle the new land. He returned to Green-land with a group of followers who increased in numbers over the years. Two main settlements were founded: one, *Ill. 55* centred on Erik's farm at Brattahlid (Qagssiarssuk) in Eriksfjord, was known as the Eastern settlement; the other, further north, round the modern Godthåb, was known as the Western settlement. The land was rich in wild life, in seals, in fish, whales and sea-birds; there was a little pasture and, as long as the fur and walrus ivory could be exported to Europe, the future of the new land

55 The site of Erik the Red's settlement at Brattahlid in Greenland. The walls seen in the photograph belong to later medieval buildings. Brattahlid (nowadays known as Qagssiarssuk) was the centre of the southernmost Viking settlement of Greenland and from here Erik's son, Leif, set out on his American expedition

was assured. A cathedral was established in the Eastern settlement at Gardar (Igaliko), a monastery and a nunnery were founded, and twelve parish churches functioned in this settlement at the height of Greenland's prosperity. It has been calculated that at its greatest period some three thousand people lived in the two main settlements. The sad story of the rise, decline and eventual fall in the late fifteenth century of medieval Greenland cannot be told here as most of the story lies outside the period covered by this book. At the end of the Viking period Greenland was an established area of settlement looking for the expansion of its economy to the unknown and as yet unexplored districts of the North (a runic inscription of 1333 at Kingigtorssuaq, between latitude 72° and 73°N *Ill. 56* records how three Norse-Greenlanders had wintered there). Excavations in Greenland by Danish archaeologists have revealed much of this later medieval settlement in some detail, but little has been revealed of the Viking period proper, save for some buildings at Brattahlid, of which only one is documented – the eleventh-century church of Thjodhild. This had curved walls of turf and was very small – about 2 m. × 3·75 m.

56 The runic inscription on a small blackish-green stone, 10 cm. long, discovered in 1824 at Kingigtorssuaq near Upernavik, northern Greenland. It reads: 'Erling Sighvatsson and Bjarni Thordarson and Eindridi O[dd]sson on the Saturday before the minor Rogation day piled these cairns and cleared . . .' The three cairns still survive

The Discovery of America

Bjarni Herjolfsson discovered America by accident about 985. Bjarni had returned home from Norway to Iceland to find that his parents had left to settle with Erik the Red. He decided to join them with his companions and set out. 'Our voyage', he said, 'will seem foolhardy, since not one of us has ever sailed into the Greenland Sea.'

Nevertheless they set out immediately they were ready and sailed three days before losing sight of land. Then their following wind failed, and north winds and fogs overtook them, so that they did not know where they were going. This continued over many days . . . before sighting land. They wondered among themselves what land this could be. Bjarni said that he thought it could not be Greenland . . . 'I think we should sail close in to the land.' This they did, and could soon see that this was not a mountainous land, but wooded and with low hills . . . Bjarni's men asked him if this was Greenland; he said that he did not think so . . . 'for there are said to be huge glaciers in Greenland'.

Bjarni never actually landed in America but turned back to Greenland, and it was left to Leif, son of Erik the Red, to land in North America and give names to it: *Helluland*, *Markland* and *Vinland*. The story of these and subsequent voyages are told in the sagas of the Greenlanders and of Erik the Red and in one or two other less coherent sources.

While there can be no doubt that the Vikings discovered America or indeed that some Vikings spent some time there – it is recorded, for example, that Thorvald, Leif's brother, lived there for two years until he was killed by the local inhabitants – and may have meant to settle in the country, opinions differ widely concerning alleged Viking antiquities discovered on the North American continent. Much of this evidence can be dismissed as of no account; the Newport tower on Rhode Island has been thought to be a Viking structure, but is exactly paralleled by a seventeenth-century English windmill; the runic stone from Kensington in North Minnesota was faked by a local farmer of Swedish descent; the find of Norwegian weapons from a site at Beardmore, near Lake Nipigon, in Ontario in 1930 was almost certainly salted by a Lt. Jens Bloch. The publication of the so-called Vinland Map amongst much ballyhoo in 1965, apparently provided a fifteenth-century parchment map of the north Atlantic which showed the east coast of Canada and a startlingly accurate map of Greenland. A Latin text records that the companions of Bjarni and Lir discovered Vinland. Spectrographic analysis of the ink, however, showed traces of a modern chemical (anatase) unknown before the First World War. The map is, therefore, a forgery, although persistent efforts are made in the face of the evidence (as with the Kensington stone) to claim its authenticity.

Other minor evidence must be dismissed; but a site excavated by the Norwegian author, Helge Ingstad, and his archaeologist wife at L'Anse aux Meadows in northern

Newfoundland has at last produced a site dated, by the radiocarbon method, to the Viking Age. Two finds of objects from the site – a spindle-whorl, for weighting the spindle for spinning wool, and a ring-headed pin – are the only movable objects of Viking Age date found on the site. The building types are related to those in the Scandinavian settlements. This site must be considered as the permanent settlement of a group of Vikings who probably lived in this area in the eleventh century. They can certainly not be identified with any known historical character and least of all with Leif Erikson, who wintered one year at a place he named *Leifsbuðir*.

The only other find of an antiquity of the Viking Age in North America (and the only one from the United States) which bears serious consideration is a Norwegian coin discovered during amateur excavations at Naskeag Point on the coast of Maine. The coin – which is of a rare type – was issued during the reign of Olav Kyrre at some date between 1065–80. It is said that we have no exact evidence as to its exact find circumstances, but the balance of professional opinion seems to accept the idea that the coin reached the coast of Maine in the early medieval period.

That the Vikings discovered America is accepted by all but a few scholars who insist that Irish priests got there before them. Nothing should detract from the Viking achievement in this direction, and yet neither the Vikings nor the rest of the known world were able to utilize this discovery. The lines of communication were too long, there was richer economic potential nearer at hand in Iceland and Greenland, they adventured only along the coast – perhaps as far south as New England – and up one or two rivers, into a few inlets, and could not use the potential which they saw there. They had neither the wealth, the people, nor the organization to develop these new lands and, while the achievements of Bjarni and Leif were never quite forgotten in northern Europe, they achieved a legendary-like quality which was not even known to the merchant venturers of Genoa and the Mediterranean in the late fifteenth century. In 1347 (less than 150 years before the voyage of Columbus!) Icelandic annals record the last remarkable event concerning Markland, and thereafter Scandinavian contacts with America are unrecorded.

The Sea

The Viking achievement in the West was only accomplished as a result of fine seamanship and skilful shipbuilding. The great ships preserved in Oslo and Roskilde are amongst the most impressive remains of the Viking Age: no one can stand unmoved in the Viking Ship Museum in Oslo, for the skill of the shipwrights eleven hundred years ago produced in the Gokstad ship an *Ill. 61* object of admiration for all sea-going people.

It has been suggested above that the sail was perhaps introduced into northern waters before the Viking period, but in the ninth century we have positive proof of the sailing-ship in the great vessels found in the graves of southern Norway, Tune, Oseberg and Gokstad. The Gokstad ship is the most impressive of these vessels, at once a symbol of wealth and power and of the potentiality of the Viking in the western seas. An exact copy of the Gokstad ship sailed in 1893 to the U.S.A., as a pointed reminder to the Americans (who were celebrating Columbus's fourth centenary) of previous visits to their shores, and the experienced master, Captain Magnus Andersen, who commanded this copy could not praise her too highly:

. . . we often had the pleasure of darting through the water at speeds of 10, and sometimes even 11, knots. This in spite of a primitive and relatively small rigging! Whether the old Norsemen used their ships in the same

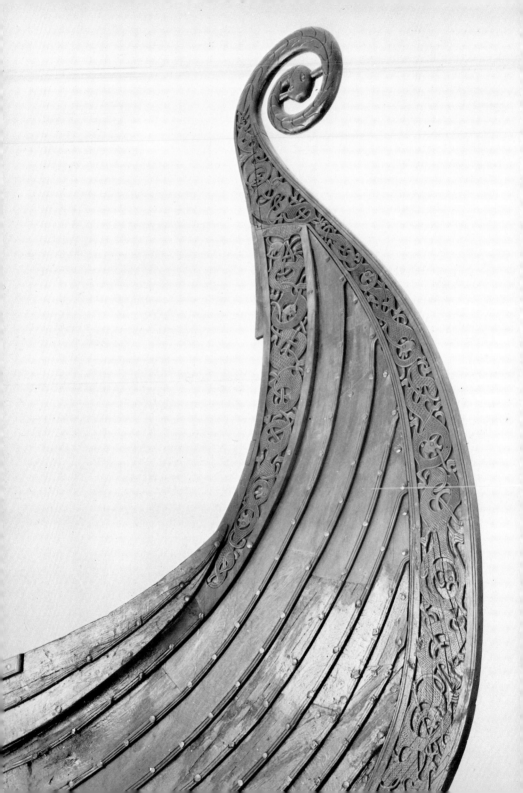

way as this is hard to say, but it does not seem unlikely that they used the ships for all they were worth. It seems absolutely certain that in those days too they wished to travel as fast as possible; why else should they have taken the trouble to improve the structure until it was so perfect that not even the shipbuilders of our time can do better as far as the ship's bottom is concerned. The fact is that the finest merchant-ships of our day, those regarded as the best sailers, have practically the same type of bottom as the Viking ships.

Many types of vessels were used by the Scandinavians in the Viking period. The rowing-boat (*bátr*) was usually distinguished by the number of oars, a *færæringr* for example had four. The chief vessel for coastal and shallow waters was the *karfi* and this was sometimes used as a warship. The true warship, however, was the long ship (*langskip*), but it may have been difficult in many ways to distinguish this from the *hafskip*, or sea-going vessel, which is sometimes known as a merchant vessel (*kaupskip*). Ships could be used for many purposes and it is difficult to give the Gokstad ship a specific label; *langskip* would cover the weapons found in it, though its sea-going qualities would justify labelling it as a *hafskip*, but perhaps it would be better described as a general-duties vessel.

The Gokstad ship is the best documented of the Viking *Ills 60, 61* ships, and a description of it will serve as a guide to the type of vessel used in the Viking Age. Slight typological

57 The highly decorated prow of the Oseberg ship. This vessel was probably used in coastal waters by a king or chieftain. A woman's body was, however, found in the grave

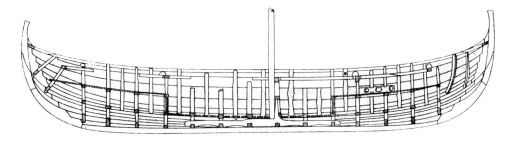

58, 59 Preliminary reconstructions by Olaf Oslen and Ole Crumlin-Pedersen of wrecks 1 and 3 from Skuldelev, near Roskilde, Denmark; two of five block-ships sunk in the eleventh century. Each vessel had a well for cargo amidships and oar-holes only at prow and stern, where the vessels were decked. Note the tiller of the lateral steering oar at the stern

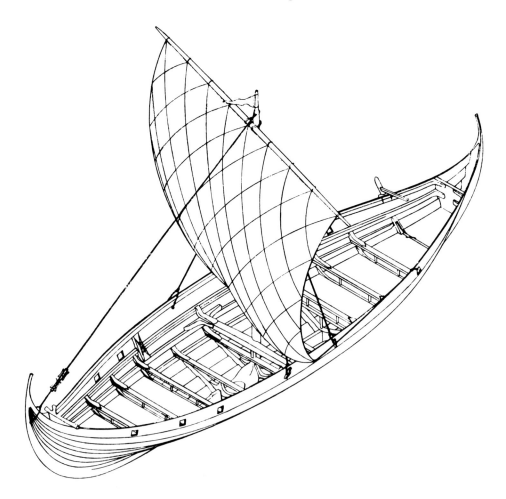

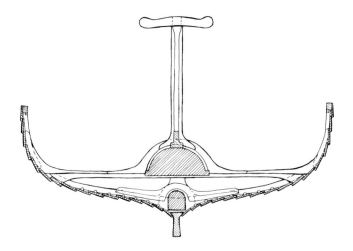

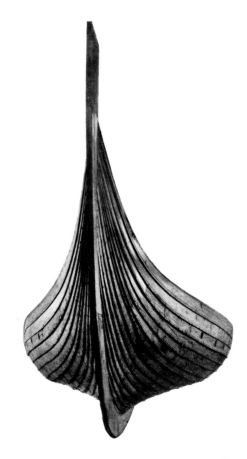

60, 61 Section through the Gokstad ship
and view of the prow of the vessel. The
clinkered construction is clearly seen and
in the third plank below the gunwale are
the oar-holes, which would be closed by
small internal shutters when the ship was
under sail. The upright T-shaped feature
amidships is one of a pair of crutches
which would carry spars and possibly
even the mast, when this was unstepped.
In this position the spars would form a
ridge for a tent which would be erected
when the ship was hove-to at night. The
immense size of the mast-fish at deck
level and of the mast-seating on the keel
are clearly seen in the section and some
impression of the size of the keel itself
can be gained from the photograph. This
was a much more workman-like vessel
than the coastal vessel found at Oseberg
(*Ill. 57*) and must have been used as a
general purpose sea-going ship. A copy
of the Gokstad ship sailed the Atlantic
in 1892

Ills 58, 59

advances can be seen as the Viking Age progresses and ships of later date, like those raised from the bed of Roskilde fjord (used to block one of the approaches to the town of Roskilde in the early eleventh century), the Swedish finds from Galtabäck and Falsterbo (dated by radiocarbon analysis to the late eleventh and early twelfth centuries), enable us to follow certain changes of the design throughout this period. At either end of the scale ships like those from Kvalsund, discussed above, and thirteenth-century vessels or fragments from Asker and Bergen in Norway enable us to view the whole sequence of northern shipbuilding.

Ills 60, 61

The Gokstad ship is built of oak – only the decking, mast, yards and oars are of pine. It is 23·3 m. overall and 5·25 m. amidships. With a load of 8 tons it would draw approximately 74 cm., a draught which might increase to 92 cm. when fully loaded. The keel, which is made of a single T-shaped piece of timber, is joined to members at either end which rise to form prow and stern-posts which possibly terminated in a curving tip. It is clinker-built, the planks overlapping each other and being lashed to the rather slight ribs of the vessel by pliable roots of spruce. Cross-beams above the water-line, supported on inverted L-shaped pieces of timber, tied the whole vessel together. The third plank below the gunwale was pierced by oar-holes which were closed when the vessel was under way. The planks were nailed together by iron rivets clenched over washers. The mast was seated in a housing of great blocks of wood attached to the keel; it was probably about 10 m. long and could be easily raised or lowered. The sail was carried on a single yard, 11 m. long, and was of white wool with sewn-on red stripes. The oars were probably only used in inland water for manœuvring in harbour or in adverse weather conditions. It was steered by a large oar attached to the starboard (literally: steering side) side of the stern. With the vessel were found a large number of pieces of shipboard equipment – anchor, gangplank, spars and bailers.

This was a light vessel, and the method of attachment of the planks to the ribs gave her an elasticity which enabled her to rise to the waves without the structure being too badly shaken.

As time went on the form of the Viking ships developed, but in general terms did not differ greatly from that of the Gokstad vessel. The stepping of the mast, for example, seems to have become more efficient in the course of the Viking Age; the keelson becoming longer, until, in the Middle Ages, its length approached that of the keel itself.

The navigational practices of the Viking Age have been much discussed. To a large extent their ships were sailed within sight of land, but when ships crossed the seas to the Western Isles, to Iceland or to America, some form of navigational aid must have been used. Presumably the stars and the sun were used in such a context, and there is some evidence that bearing dials and azimuth tables were used as further aids. The Vikings seem to have had a fair idea of latitude, but none of longitude; they probably used a method of reckoning, known from later periods, by means of which they would sail to the latitude of their destination and then follow this parallel until land was sighted. On well-known passages, like that to the Faroes, they were probably able to sail by an almost direct route.

Land Transport

We are so fascinated by the ships of the Vikings that it is easy to forget that they also travelled great distances by land. The trade route from Uppland in Sweden to Tröndelag in Norway, for instance, was not negotiated by ships but by horses, sledges and even carts, while the *Ills 63, 65* great ox-road south from the north of Jutland into Germany was used widely, presumably by quite sophisticated forms of transport. In winter, passage over snow

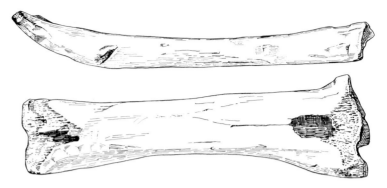

62, 63 *Above*, bone skate from grave 573 at Birka, and from the metacarpal of a horse. The Norse word for a skate *ísleggr*, means literally 'ice-leg-bone'. Skates of this form are, however, found throughout western Europe. *Below*, the base of the 'simple' sledge from the Viking ship-burial from Oseberg, Norway. To it was fastened a plain, box-like body

Ill. 62
Ill. 64

and ice was fast, and the presence of large numbers of skates in the archaeological levels at the Swedish town of Birka indicates the importance of travel on ice, as does the presence of iron spikes which could be attached to a horse's hooves so that they would not slip on the frozen lake.

The horse was important. Bridles, spurs, saddles and (for the first time) stirrups are found in archaeological contexts, while horseshoes are mentioned in Icelandic texts. For the horse as a pack animal we must rely on the literary evidence. One such source, *Grettis Saga*, tells of a man buying 'much fish and carrying it away on seven horses.' The horse was used as a draught animal as can be

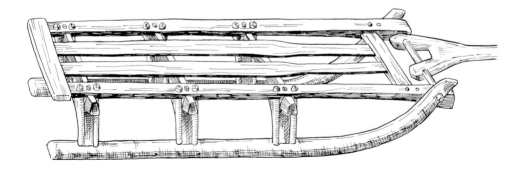

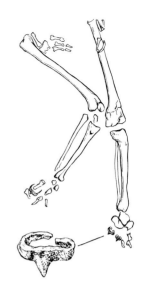

64 Spikes were attached to a horse's feet to facilitate riding on snow or ice. The spikes were of iron and these examples were found at the feet of a horse in a grave at Birka. Birka itself lies on an island which is easily approached in winter over the frozen lake

seen from pictorial representations on tapestry and stones. Horse-collars are found in Denmark, but whether oxen or horses were used to pull the ceremonial wooden wagon *Ill. 98* found in the Oseberg ship-burial, or the carts which made the ruts on the road revealed in the Lindholm excavations, is not known.

From the same Norwegian grave at Oseberg, which provided us with a wagon, come a series of sledges which *Ill. 63* have bodies attached to the runners by means of struts. Earlier, at the beginning of our era, dug-out sledges are known; these were presumably used for transporting goods on snow or grass. Similar sledges undoubtedly continued in use for a considerable period; their function

65 Detail of the ornament of a memorial stone from Alskog, Gotland, Sweden, portraying a wagon. On the only surviving Viking example, the funerary cart from Oseberg (*Ill. 69*), the axle-trees are connected by a beam, and it also had spoked wheels and a pair of shafts connected by a chain

was probably entirely different from that of the frame sledges found at Oseberg, which would be used almost exclusively on snow. But for simple transport on snow, skis and skates were used. Skates, indeed, were already being used in sporting contexts, and as a test of general manly prowess: in the *Heimskringla*, for example, one man says to another, 'I was so skilful on skates that no one could beat me, and you could no more do it than an ox.'

Trade and Towns

The westward adventures of the Vikings were largely caused by a search for wealth, either in the form of goods or land. The distinction between the pirate and the merchant is a fine one and it is to the latter activity that we must now turn our attention, for the mechanics of trade were responsible for the eastern expansion which some would see as resulting in the foundation of the Russian state and which brought to Scandinavia wealth and to spare from the Arab and Byzantine worlds. As we have seen, throughout the first millennium the population of Scandinavia had traded over long distances; in the Roman Iron Age a vast quantity of luxury items were brought into the North, while for much of the succeeding four hundred years trade, even if it fluctuated, was always there, bringing wealth from the South and East to the men of the North. During the Viking period this trade grew and prospered, and the establishment of towns and major market-places is symptomatic of this activity. Helgö in the heart of the rich kingdom of Uppland was succeeded by the greatest of all the Viking market-places, Birka, a trading station with all the attributes of a town, as we can learn from the western European sources which describe journeys to this teeming metropolis by the first missionaries to the North. The site of Birka is well known from both literary and archaeological sources. It is on an island in the great Mälar lake, which pushes into the heart of

66 General view of part of the grave-field outside the defences of the Viking town of Birka, Sweden. Some 1200 graves, out of an estimated 2000, have been excavated here, mostly by Hjalmar Stolpe in the late nineteenth century. They produced by far the richest finds of any Scandinavian cemetery of the Viking period, demonstrating connections with the Arab and Byzantine world, as well as with western Europe

Uppland from the Baltic Sea, and lies on the route from the royal centre of Uppsala to the outside world. Within a semicircular bank, probably originally capped by wooden battlements, is a 29-acre site in the centre of which, by the water's edge, is an area of settlement, known as 'the Black Earth' because of the colour of its soil. The whole site is dominated by a fort which is built outside the line of the wall. Only a small area of this enclosure has been investigated archaeologically; we know very little of its appearance, of the shape of its houses, of its street system; all we have is evidence of industry – bone, pottery, metalworking, jewellery. Excavations are planned which should uncover more of the town, whose importance is indicated by the 1,200 graves *Ill. 66* outside the walls. These graves, excavated in the last century, show that the town flourished from about 800 to 950/975, and that it had commercial connections with all the known world, particularly with the East. Coins, pottery, metalwork, skins, silks, glass and other objects found here, demonstrate a lively contact with Britain, with the Carolingian and Byzantine empires, with the caliphates of western Asia, with Russia, with the Lapps and with the other Scandinavian kingdoms. Inside the walls of this town the merchants would meet to bargain: Frisians, Swedes, Britons, Germans, perhaps even Arabs, would gather to trade under the protection of the King's representative and buy the goods produced by the local inhabitants – antler combs, jewellery, leather goods, as well as food and drink. They would come by sea, tying up their ship in one of the harbours outside the town or drawing it up on to the shallow beach inside the walls which was protected by a palisade of stakes set in the water: in the winter traders would come by skis, skates and sledge over the frozen lake. For nearly two centuries this was the most northerly major mercantile centre of Europe.

There were, however, other towns – other markets. Some were small, perhaps even seasonal camps, dealing with local trade or with merchants seeking a specific type of goods. In certain parts of Norway, for instance, there was a specialized industry which produced soapstone bowls and other vessels, which were apparently in 'great demand throughout Scandinavia and would be sold at the markets. Other towns within the Viking sphere of influence were large and flourishing – bigger even than *Ill. 67* Birka. Such a town was Hedeby on the neck of the Jutland Peninsula; planted on the edge of the Schlei fjord it had easy and protected access to the sea. Excavations within the great bank of this town have revealed mercantile contacts similar to those found at Birka. This was a

67 Aerial view of the Viking town of Hedeby in north Germany showing very clearly the embanked defences of the final stages of the town. The town was familiar to contemporary chroniclers in both east and west. It is mentioned by King Alfred and by the Anglo-Saxon chronicler Æthelweard who, in the late tenth century, described it as a town, 'which is called Sleswic by the Saxons, and Haithaby by the Danes'. The town was destroyed *c.* 1050 and refounded a few miles away as the modern Schleswig

town mentioned by two travellers at the English court of Alfred the Great – an Anglo-Saxon, Wulfstan, and a Norwegian, Ohthere – they called it *Hæðum* and they had both traded there. Another town mentioned by Ohthere was *Sciringesheal,* in the south of Norway, five days' sailing from Hedeby. *Sciringesheal* has been identified by Norwegian historians and archaeologists as Kaupang (*lit.* 'market') in Tjölling, Vestfold. Kaupang is now set on a shallow bay, between rocky hills; in the Viking Age, when the sea-level was six feet higher, it was a natural harbour protected by a string of islands and shoals. Since, moreover, the market-place had a natural defence of hills, there was no need for the bank encountered at Birka and Hedeby. Excavation here has again produced many imported goods, although objects of eastern origin are

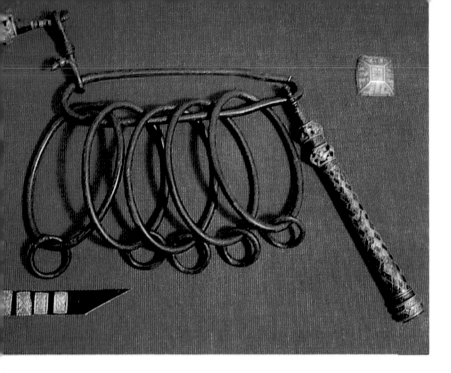

68–70 Finds from the Oseberg ship-burial, Norway. *Above*, a rider's rattle from the great ship-burial together with a number of mounts from a bridle. The elaborate wagon, *below*, is carved with scenes which have been interpreted in the light of our knowledge of Scandinavian mythology. The wagon was probably built for ceremonial purposes. *Opposite*, a detail of the frame of the Oseberg wagon

comparatively rare. Kaupang was obviously not so rich as the other two towns, but it must have been one of the main outlets of trade for Vestfold, one of the richest areas in Norway.

Other towns are known to have been founded in Scandinavia in the course of the Viking Age, but not all have been investigated thoroughly; Västergarn on Gotland, for example. Other towns, such as Sigtuna and Lund, seem to have developed later; these functioned not only as local market-places but also as cult places, administrative centres and, with the coming of Christianity, as episcopal sees. The Vikings also founded towns and trading stations in the colonies. Dublin was founded by the Vikings in the 830s; originally it was a fortified base and administrative centre; it later became an extremely important port, its international character being hinted at in Arabic, Norse, English and Irish sources. Excavations in Dublin are beginning to uncover an important industrial area of the Viking town, one of the cemeteries of which (at Islandbridge, Kilmainham) has been known for many years. The Vikings founded other towns in Ireland, but in England and elsewhere they took over existing towns. Some, like Dorestad in Holland, were already considerable trading centres, others, like York, were given a more mercantile character than they had hitherto had.

In eastern Europe the pre-Viking Scandinavians already had considerable economic interests on the south coast of the Baltic. One of their sites there – Grobin, near Liepaja (Libau) in western Latvia – was investigated by a Swedish archaeologist between the wars: it seems to have been a town of para-military character under the control of soldiers from central Sweden, but functioning, nevertheless, as a trading station. By the early years of the ninth century the Vikings were in control of a North Russian *Ill. 78* town, Staraja Ladoga, which they might even have

71 Silver coin probably struck in the Viking town of Hedeby in the early years of the ninth century. This coin represents the earliest native coinage of Scandinavia

founded. The complicated story of Swedish-Russian relations is discussed below; suffice it to say here that trade is practically the whole basis of the Viking activities in the East.

Internal trade also flourished. Into Scandinavia poured silver and gold, rare spices, silks and fine woollen cloth, wine and exotic bronzes; but the market which supplied the Frisian merchant with slaves, furs, ropes and honey also supplied the local farmer with his iron knife and the salt to preserve his meat. Internal trade could be on a fairly large scale, iron and soapstone, apparently transported over great distances, being two materials particularly in demand in the home market. To a certain extent this trade could not have existed without a standard of exchange; this was silver – either in the form of coin or as bullion. Although there was a reasonably satisfactory Scandinavian currency from time to time, there was no *Ill. 71* real monetary economy until the end of the Viking period; the merchant relied on the weight of the silver he received and among the commonest antiquities found in merchant graves – as in earlier periods – are small pairs of portable *Ill. 32* scales, which would be used in the market-place to check the silver in any transaction. Perhaps because there was no effective royal control of currency in the tenth and eleventh centuries, vast quantities of foreign coin circulated in Scandinavia. We have seen that Viking Age hoards in Sweden yielded 30,000 Anglo-Saxon coins; there are also 52,000 Arabic coins and 58,500 Frankish or German coins. Although the Danish and Norwegian totals do not by any means measure up to these – there are less than 3,000 Anglo-Saxon coins recorded from Norway and only 5,300 from Denmark – the importance of silver to the Scandinavians cannot be underestimated. The fact that silver was treated as bullion is emphasized by the fact *Ill. 72* that many of the hoards contain pieces of broken and cut silver (hack-silver), often bits of old or outmoded jewellery or plate, cut into pieces for the purpose of trade. It may be assumed that the Vikings accepted coins at their face value in its country of origin (where rigorous standards were imposed) and by weight at home, where the coins themselves were often cut to balance the scales.

The Vikings in Russia and Beyond

It has been shown how, since the Roman Iron Age, the Scandinavians had been in intermittent contact with the eastern Mediterranean by way of the great rivers of Eastern Europe. Viking presence in Russia is denied by nobody, but for nearly two hundred years argument – based on nationalism – as to the importance of this presence has been raging fiercely. There are two schools of thought, that of the *Normanists* (mainly Scandinavians) and that of the *anti-Normanists* (mainly Russian): the Normanists believe that the Vikings founded the great towns of European Russia and hence laid the foundation of the Russian state; the anti-Normanists hold that the Russian state is of Slav origin. Although the anti-Normanists have been the most virulent, the Normanists have themselves quite often been unreasonable. While tending to an acceptance of the Normanist viewpoint, I am not swayed too greatly by some of their more resounding statements. The roots of the problem lie in the identity of a people called *Rus* who appear in the Russian Primary Chronicle (*Povest Vremennykh Let*). Between 860 and 862, according to the Chronicle, the inhabitants of central European Russia invited a number of men 'who were known as *Rus* just as some are known as

72 In the excavation of the Black Earth at Birka was found this iron dish together with a large number of silver objects – penannular brooches, armrings, bangles and coins. The coins date the deposition of the hoard to *c.* 975 and symbolize the end of the once rich and prosperous town which is now an empty meadow covered with juniper scrub

Swedes, others Northmen, others Angles (*i.e.* from Angeln in South Jutland) and others Goths (*i.e.* from Gotland), to bring order to their country'. Three brothers came: Rurik, the eldest, settled in Novgorod, while the others (who died within a few years) settled in Beloozero and Izborsk. 'On account of these *Varangians* [Scandinavians] the district of Novgorod became known as the land of the Rus.' This is merely a summary of a complicated story told by a later chronicler who was more than

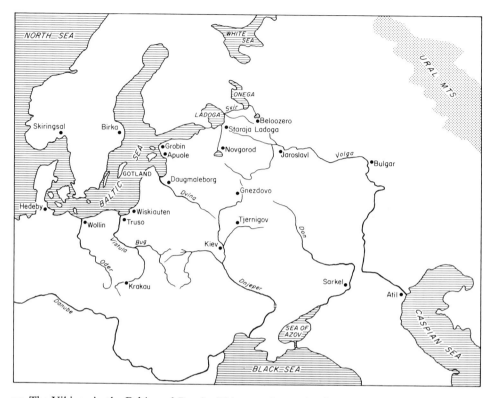

73 The Vikings in the Baltic and Russia. This map shows the rivers which formed their main trade routes

a little muddled by geographical terms and historical events, indeed the word Varangian itself was not apparently used until the tenth century. The origin of the word *Rus* has not been satisfactorily explained, although it has been alternatively suggested that the word is derived from the Finnish *Ruotsi*, or from the Old Norse *ródr* (a rowing-way), or again that these men came from Roslagen in Uppland, Sweden. The way they are described in the Russian Chronicle in the company of other Scandinavian people would imply their northern origins, while the lively tradition that they founded the great city states of Russia (particularly Novgorod and Kiev), which is strongly attested in other sources both eastern and western, is hard to gainsay. How long they retained their Scandinavian character is, however, quite another matter.

The Vikings came to Russia for purposes of trade, long before Rurik was invited to Novgorod, and they developed there two major routes, one along the Dnjeper *Ill. 73* and the other along the Volga. The former is described by the Russian Primary Chronicler: 'Starting from the Greeks, this route proceeds along the Dnjeper, above which a portage leads to the Lovat. By following the Lovat, the great lake Ilmen is reached. The river Volkhov which flows out of this lake enters the great lake Nevo [Ladoga], which opens into the Varangian [Baltic] Sea.' It was along this route that the great towns of Kiev, Smolensk (or its predecessor), Novgorod and Staraja Ladoga are situated, and it is along this route that quite a considerable body of Viking archaeological material has been assembled. The second route exploited by the Vikings was to the east, and here there was no possibility of settlement on the same scale, as large towns had long been established to control the fur trade; this control was

74 Part of a hoard of silver rings and bangles from Asarve, Hemse, Gotland. The whole hoard weighs almost 9 kg.

75 The so-called sword of St Stephen in the cathedral treasury at Prague. The ivory mounts are decorated in the Mammen style (*see* p. 126 f.)

exercised by the rulers of the Bulgars and Khazars in the region of the Volga, who charged a toll on traders. From the Bulgar bend it was possible for the traders to strike out across the desert to reach the silk route to Baghdad and China somewhere near the Aral Sea. Though the documentation is scanty, Arab sources and archaeological finds encourage the belief that it was of some importance, and it was probably along this route, rather than through Byzantium, that many of the Arabic coins found in Scandinavia had travelled. It was probably in this area that the Vikings came into contact with Arab writers such as Ibn Fadlán who gives the first graphic descriptions of the *Rus* and of their strange customs. A third, but less dramatic, eastern trade route passed down the Oder and Neisse to link up with the great east–west trade route from Mainz to Kiev by way of Cracow, and to the Danube and the rich markets of South-central Europe and the Mediterranean.

Excavations at Novgorod, Staraja Ladoga and Kiev, as well as at Gnezdovo (the cemetery of the precursor of Smolensk), have produced some Scandinavian material, but not in sufficient quantities to enable us to form major judgements concerning the pattern or chronology of the *Ill. 78* Viking incursion. At Staraja Ladoga, the only town in which major ninth-century levels have been reached, the evidence is equivocal as the foundations of the buildings excavated seem to be of Finnish rather than Scandinavian character. At the Gnezdovo cemetery a fair amount of Scandinavian material has been recovered – although Russian archaeologists would say that the amount is minimal. *Ill. 76* At Novgorod only a small area of the original town has yet been excavated and only in one portion of this has any ninth-century material been recovered. Nevertheless Novgorod was thoroughly influenced by the Vikings. As late as the eleventh century a Swedish rune-master was inscribing the name Novgorod (Holmgarðr) on a

76 The medieval Russian city of Novgorod. Since the war excavations have been carried out on the kremlin side of the river (the kremlin, or fortress, is in the centre of the west bank of the river). Finds here are completely Slav in character and it is possible that the earlier settlement, of which traces have been found, was on the eastern bank. Novgorod may have been founded by the Vikings, in the ninth century. It certainly had Viking rulers at that time. The numbers indicate the sites of excavations

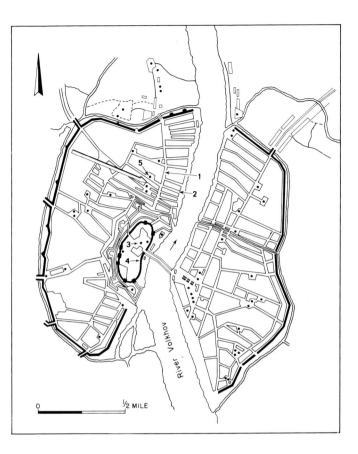

77 Silver brooch from Jelets, Voronez, USSR, one of a number of objects decorated in the Borre style found in European Russia. Some objects decorated thus, may have been made in Russia itself, but many, like this one, were almost certainly made in central Sweden. Actual size

78 The excavations at the important north Russian trading station of Staraja Ladoga. This town was almost certainly under the control of the Swedes in the early ninth century, but the 'block houses' seen here are of an east Baltic or Slav type

Ill. 83 memorial stone at Sjusta, Skokloster, Uppland, in an inscription in memory of four men, one of whom, Spjallbude, 'died in Holmgarðr in Olaf's church'. The fact that there was a church dedicated to the Scandinavian royal saint Olaf in Novgorod in the eleventh century speaks volumes for the Swedish presence there.

But, as in Normandy and in England, the Scandinavian settlers in Russia quickly adapted their lives to that of the Slav tribes among whom they were living; the fact that the houses discovered at Ladoga are built in a Finnish style is no more significant than the fact that when they came to England the Vikings erected crosses of an Anglo-

79 Cross of poor quality silver from a grave at Norsborg, Botkyrka, Södermanland, Sweden. The cross is of a type made for the Slav-Byzantine church of south Russia

Saxon form over the graves of their dead. The Vikings of Ladoga were traders not craftsmen: when they wished to build a house they employed local labour, and the local labour-force built in the native tradition. The foundation and control of Novgorod, Smolensk and Kiev were necessary to the security of one of the major routes to the East, and the importance of this to the Vikings is emphasized by the fact that most of the seven major rapids on the Dnjeper bear names of Scandinavian origin. As long as the rulers of the great towns maintained amicable relations with their Scandinavian cousins it would not matter how slavicized they became. In a town largely peopled by slaves, artisans, craftsmen and merchants who would be Slav and where the only Scandinavians would be a few strong-arm characters among the riff-raff of the ruler's bodyguard, it would soon be inevitable that the leading men of Kiev and Novgorod would adopt the major elements of Slav civilization and the orthodox religion of the Byzantine Eastern Empire. However, even as late as the eleventh century, one of the greatest of the Kievan princes, Yaroslav, was conscious enough of his Scandinavian heritage to marry the daughter of Olaf Skötkonung, King of Sweden, and give hospitality to the exiled Harald Haraldsson (Harald Hardrada) of Norway, who later became King of Norway and was to suffer defeat and death at the hands of the Anglo-Saxon King Harold at Stamford Bridge in 1066.

Trade was not, however, the only reason for the Vikings' eastward journeys. At all times the Viking was a mercenary soldier of skill and loyalty who fought for reward wherever he could find employment. Having been brought up in a heroic tradition he was willing to fight and die for the man he chose as lord, whatever that man's nationality. On many of the Swedish rune-stones from the ninth century onwards there are references to men who died 'eastwards in Greece' (*i.e.* Byzantium) or in

80–83 *Above* and *below, left*, runic inscription on a boulder from Ed, near Stockholm, which was cut to the order of a man who had been 'leader of the host' in the Byzantine empire. *Below, right*, and *opposite*, stones with runic inscriptions from Sjusta, Skokloster, Uppland and Kålsta, Häggeby, Uppland

84 Marble lion removed in the Middle Ages from the Piraeus (the port of Athens) to Venice. On its shoulder is a runic inscription of familiar Swedish style, now unfortunately illegible but demonstrating the eastern travels of the Vikings

Ills 80, 81 Russia. At Ed, near Stockholm, was found a long inscription:

> Ragnvald had the runes cut in memory of his mother Fastvi, Onäm's daughter. She died in Ed. God help her soul. Ragnvald had the runes cut, he was in Greece, he was the leader of the host.

This surely refers to the Norse mercenaries, the Varangian Guard, who served the Emperor in Constantinople (Miklagarðr): Ragnvald, a man of high birth, had reason to boast if he had commanded these crack troops. By the middle of the eleventh century the Varangian Guard had ceased to be a specifically Scandinavian institution; other foreigners, English and French, were converting it to a kind of foreign legion. As the Varangian Guard lost its Viking character, so the Scandinavian connections with the East gradually declined, only the rune-stones telling us of a continuous contact until at least 1060.

Chapter Four

The Vikings at Home

In considering the great adventures of the Vikings overseas it is easy to forget their presence in their homeland, where they enjoyed the fruits of their external contact, whether mercantile or piratical. In general it is true to say that the Scandinavians of the Viking Age were not fundamentally different from their ancestors who have been described earlier in this book. The Viking who had travelled outside his homeland was different only in outlook from the home-bound Scandinavian of the Migration or Vendel period. The tenor of life at home was very much the same, the economy was basically agrarian, the sea and the lakes provided food, houses were built, cloth woven, children born; people prospered or failed to prosper, as did their forebears. There seems to have been no dramatic economic change in Scandinavian life inside the homeland around 800. For one reason or another the Viking adventure overseas began about then, but people's lives were little affected by these developments.

The social structure of Viking society conformed to a norm well known in contemporary Europe, a norm which can be explained with misleading simplicity. At the bottom of the social scale was the slave (*þræll*), a term which covered a wide class of men from a bankrupt to a captive in war; the son of a slave was also a slave. At home he was employed on the farm; he represented capital to his owner and could be sold abroad without difficulty in the markets of Europe and the East. The life of a slave was of no account, and it is by no means unknown to find a sacrificed slave in a Scandinavian grave

85, 86 Skull of a woman showing the blow which killed her. She was buried as a sacrifice in the mound seen *opposite*; her skeleton lay on the upper of the two shelves of earth, seen in *Ill. 86*, above the coffin of a ninth-century Viking warrior. The mound, which is here seen during excavation, was at Ballateare, Isle of Man

Ills 85, 86 – an excavation at Ballateare in the Isle of Man provided a clear example of this practice. The slave's life could be hard, but it paid a slave-owner to keep his possessions in good trim, and for many a Scandinavian who was a slave in his own land the life was not too animal. Gradually, through the influence of Christianity, many slaves were freed and their lot improved; eventually a slave could even earn his freedom by his own efforts.

The free peasant (*karl*) was by no means entirely free; if he had been a slave, or if his family was of slave stock, he still owed service to the family of his erstwhile master. In ideal circumstances he owned his own land, but in practice he more often hired his services to a master, or held land in exchange for service to the proprietor. His class provided craftsmen and soldiers: some were pedlars, some may even have been merchants. They had protection under the law and played some part in its administration. It was probably from this class that many of the bands of Viking marauders and traders were raised by the tough young aristocrats who financed the expeditions. The free-

men who went on these expeditions would often have been the dissatisfied younger sons who saw no chance of bettering their position on the family's holding, and who had now a chance to win wealth and even land across the sea.

The third class consisted of the aristocrat (*jarl*) or chieftain. Basically he was a warrior who had gathered a warlike band around him and united his area of the country. In the course of the Viking Age this class of society began to hold land from the king in a proto-feudal manner. This process was to some extent responsible for the proper establishment of the Scandinavian kingdoms by depriving the *jarl* of his independence – an independence that had resulted in a lust for wealth which he had previously satisfied by acts of piracy or trade. The process of centralization was hastened by the influence of the Church, which needed the support of a strong centralized power, and by the growth of merchant guilds, which introduced certain restrictive practices that hurt the freebooter. The centralized kingdom grew, developing feudal

87 Simplified plan of Vorbasse, Denmark. The village lies along a street. Eighth-century houses and hedges are in heavy black (secondary houses have a screen). Undifferentiated lines trace the Viking settlement.

0   50   100m

ideas of military service; the king imposed taxes, established and added to his own estates and hence to his private wealth.

Throughout this period the Scandinavian depended on the land for his basic livelihood. Cattle, horses, sheep and goats were bred for milk and meat; crops were planted, grown, harvested and ground to make bread, porridge and beer; fruit was collected from the forests and heaths. Farming was becoming more intensive and breeding more selective; the Norwegian farmer, for example, developed to the full the practice of transferring cattle to high pasture-lands during the summer months, as is witnessed by the greater number of burials in these mountainous areas during the Viking Age. Sheep were of great importance in the Atlantic islands and Iceland, and being hardier could often survive the winter without the flock being thinned too much. Sheiling sites were probably developed at this period.

It is difficult to trace Viking settlement patterns in the countryside. Village sites are scarce, although many scholars are willing to explain this by the assumption that the villages of the Viking Age are covered by modern settlements. In many areas, notably Iceland, Greenland and some of the colonies, there is plenty of evidence for scattered single farms, and one has the suspicion that the nucleated settlement was rare outside Denmark. A campaign of excavations at various sites in Denmark has revealed a number of villages of which the most complete is Vorbasse in Jutland. The site was first settled in the eighth Ill. 87 century and was deserted in the late Viking Age. Seven hedged plots were found, each enclosing many buildings. The site at Lindholm Høje in northern Jutland (which overlies an earlier Viking Age cemetery) has yielded the foundations of many similar houses including an eleventh-century farm built round a courtyard. This latter, which was to become the standard form of Danish farm-house in this area, is at this period only parallelled at the great Danish military sites at Trelleborg, Fyrkat and Aggersborg, where such buildings fulfilled a different function as barracks. The single-farm complex is perhaps better documented in the archaeological record, mostly in Iceland and the Atlantic isles. At Jarlshof on the southern Ill. 92 tip of the mainland of Shetland, for example, is a complex of buildings which excavation has shown to have been in continuous occupation by a Viking chieftain throughout the Viking Age. An eruption of the volcano Hekla covered some twenty early medieval farm complexes in Þjórsárdalur in Iceland. The remains of these farms show how the settlers adapted their living quarters to the raw circumstances in which they found themselves.

Soon after the establishment of the settlement it became clear to the colonists that the large rectangular house, which since the beginning of our era had been the main type of building in Scandinavia, was not suitable for the windswept island to which they had come. The great spaces were broken up and the various farm-buildings were clustered together into one irregular complex, the

88 Post in the form of an animal head, which originally was part of a piece of furniture, perhaps a chair. It was found in the ship-burial at Oseberg in south Norway. No piece of sculpture demonstrates quite so clearly the skill of the Viking craftsman working in the material – wood – with which he was most familiar. The head is decorated with Style III animals by a craftsman who has been distinguished as 'the Academician', a slightly out-of-date member of the group of artists represented in this burial, who also carved the stern of the ship (*Ill. 57*)

smithy and byre alone being built at some distance from the main farm. Large halls were not unknown in Iceland, a splendid example was revealed at the beginning of this century at Hofstaðoir, but they are rare. The houses were built of turf laid on two courses of stone, the main room lined internally with wainscotting. At one of the most typical of these farms, that at Stöng in Þjórsárdalur, the main hall had benches along each long wall on either side of a central fire-place. The main bed was in the entrance hall in an alcove and various rooms – dairies, storage

89 Bridle mount of gilt bronze from Broa, Halla, Gotland, Sweden, greatly enlarged (×2½). Here can be seen another aspect of Style III animal ornament on a different scale from that seen in the wood carving from Oseberg illustrated opposite. Other mounts from this find are depicted (actual size) in *Ills. 98–100*

90 The great axe from Mammen, Jutland, Denmark which gives its name to the Mammen style (two-thirds actual size). The axe was an important weapon of the Scandinavian warrior of the Viking period; it had symbolic aspects and was much used as a display weapon. This example is inlaid with silver wire

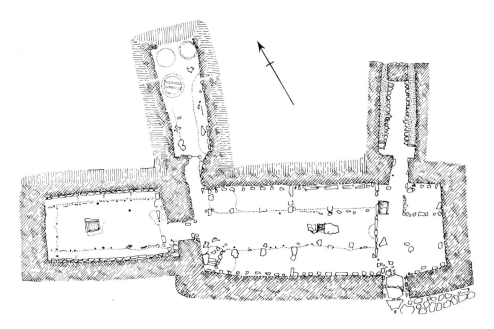

91 Plan of early medieval farm-house at Stöng, Iceland. The entrance hall leads into a pantry (or lavatory) and is separated only by a screen from the main hall with its central fire-place. On the same axis is another hall, while the dairy is set at right angles to it

space, kitchen and guest-room – were added higgledy-piggledy to the house as the need and opportunity arose.

Within houses such as these a considerable farming community lived, the slaves sleeping in the hall or in the kitchen, and most of the main activities taking place in the same two places, which were always warm. At meal-times the master of the house would sit in the 'high seat' placed at the centre of one side of the hall, and tables, perhaps in richer houses spread with a linen cloth, would be brought in. The high points of home life at this period were the great feasts, which often lasted several days. The story-telling of a skilful entertainer together with the weak beer brewed by the ladies of the house, perhaps a little imported wine, special food, and then more beer would break the monotony and isolation of the long winters of the North. In pagan times the local religious festivals were accompanied by great feasts, and the com-

92 An artist's reconstruction of the appearance of the Viking and later Norse farm, Jarlshof, which lies at the southern tip of the mainland of Shetland. As the settlement developed houses fell down and were neglected and some were put to other uses as barns and byres

ing of Christianity did not change the pattern. Other entertainments included board games and field sports of a semi-organized nature:

> . . . and people came from the west from Midfirth and from Waterness and Waterdale all the way, and from out of Longdale, and there was a great gathering together. . . . Now the sports were set going and Hall took the lead. He asked Kjartan to join in the play. . . . The game went on all day long, but no man had either the strength or litheness of limb to cope with Kjartan. And in the evenings when the games were ended, Hall stood up and said, 'It is the wish and offer of my father that those men who have come so far should stay here over night and take up the games tomorrow' . . . there were over a hundred men in the house that night. And the next day sides were divided for games again.

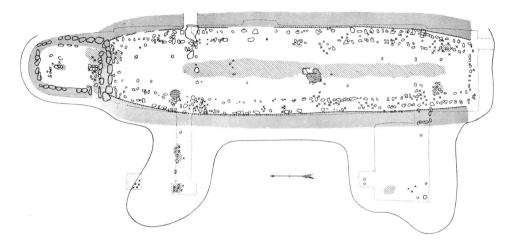

93 Plan of the large building at Hofstaðir, Iceland. It is about 45 m. long and appears to be an early version of the Icelandic farm before the addition of ancillary buildings (*cf.* Stöng, *Ill. 91*). The element 'Hof' means temple and many would see this as a pagan religious building, but in reality it has all the attributes of a domestic building of the Viking period, with lateral benches and a central fire-place in the main hall

Art

The continuity of the civilization of the North throughout the first millennium is strongly emphasized by Viking art, for the decoration applied by the Scandinavians to their everyday objects follows closely in the tradition which first emerges at the end of the Roman Iron Age. This fact so struck the French historian Marc Bloch that he used it as an illustration of the self-confidence of the Vikings in that, although they came into contact with the more sophisticated art of the Carolingian and Ottonian empires, they never let this seriously affect their own individuality. In the Viking period we see the existing animal art brought to new heights, and only with the introduction of plant ornament, towards the end of the tenth century, did their art begin to lose its vitality.

The early Viking Age provides us, by a fortunate chance, with an opportunity to witness the art of the North in its most natural medium – wood. The great ship recovered from the grave of a Viking queen or princess

94–96 *Left*, detail of the ornament of a rectangular brooch from Skabersjö, Skåne, Sweden, showing the typical ribbon-like animal of Style D; it was this late Vendel style which heralded the early Viking styles represented *right* and *below*. *Right*, a detail of the carving of an animal head-post from the Oseberg ship-burial, showing three gripping-beasts typical of the early Viking styles. *Below*, detail of the stern-post of the Oseberg ship (*cf. Ill. 57*). Two animals of Style E are interlaced together, their legs developing sometimes into tendrils which further help to bind the motif together

at Oseberg, in South Norway, is by no means as fine a sea-going vessel as that from Gokstad, but it is itself decorated with the finest ornament of Style III, and on other wooden objects in the grave are further expressions of this style which surpass anything seen in the preceding period. Two basic motifs are used in the ornament of these objects: the first is a beast with a small head, open-work panels in its hips and a frond-like extension to its limbs and to its pigtail; the second is a series of animals massed together so that the limbs constitute the most obtrusive feature, gripping the nearest element of the ornament with their paws. This motif is simplified in one of the two succeeding styles, the so-called Borre style

97 Small amber carving of a gripping-beast from Lærdal, Sogn, Norway. One of the few examples of three-dimensional carving of this style outside the Oseberg find

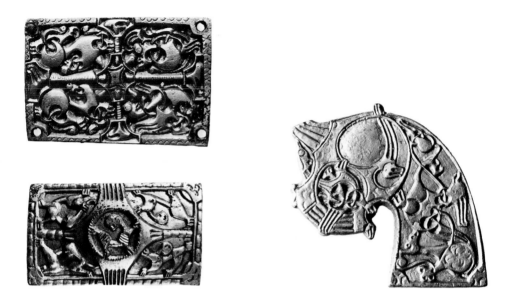

98–100 Three bronze-gilt mounts from Broa, Halla, Gotland, Sweden, one of a set of which one is illustrated in enlargement of *Ill. 89*. Two motifs are represented in the ornament of these pieces, Style E (which is seen *top left* and *right*) and the gripping-beast (which can be seen *left*). The mounts, which are illustrated at natural size, were made for a bridle. The find represents the work of one of the most competent jewellers of the Viking Age in Scandinavia

Ill. 101 – named after another rich burial. One of the main elements in this style is an animal with a head at the top of the field, the body forming a slow curve below the head to form a hip on either side. Other motifs include a specific ring-chain motif, which we encounter later in the Isle of Man, and a lion-like beast. The style emerges about the middle of the ninth century and traces linger until the end of the tenth century; it was universal in Scandinavia and particularly popular in Viking contexts in Russia.

More or less contemporary with the Borre style is the Jellinge style, which probably began towards the end of the ninth century and continued until about 1000 – dates based on coin hoards and on its occurrence in an early phase of the Viking settlement in England. It is named *Ills 102, 103* after the animal which decorates a small silver cup from the Jutland village of Jelling, the royal necropolis of

101 The three mounts from Borre, Norway, represent the three main motifs of the Borre style, *left*, a ring-chain pattern; *centre*, a backward looking animal and *right* a variety of the gripping-beast motif in which only a single creature is used

102, 103 A small silver cup from a royal grave at Jelling, Jutland, in Denmark. The animal ornament of this cup (drawn out *above*) gives its name to the Jellinge style. Note the loop or lappet at the lip, the sinuous double-contoured body of the animal and the pigtail

104 Panel of elk-horn, one of many which covered a house-shaped casket in the cathedral of Cammin in Poland. The casket was destroyed during the Second World War. It portrays a typical Mammen style animal with large spiral hips, a double contour and a billeted body, all caught up in interlace with lush acanthus-like leaves. The style takes its name from the axe seen in *Ill. 90* with which this panel should be compared

Ills 90, 104

Denmark: this animal has a ribbon-like body, a pigtail and a lip-lappet. Developing naturally out of this is the animal of the succeeding style – the Mammen style – which is a substantial creature with foliate offshoots of acanthus-leaf form, appearing at its most typical on bone and on stone. The Mammen style may be roughly dated to between 970 and 1010 and fines into the Ringerike style in which the acanthus leaf is elongated into great tendrils which often seem to take over the whole pattern – the Ringerike style is particularly popular in stone sculpture, and takes its name from a group of ornamented

105 Two of the stones from the Danish royal cemetery at Jelling in Jutland. The larger stone bears on one face an animal in the Mammen style, on another an inscription and on the third this representation of the Crucifixion – the earliest recorded in Scandinavia. The stone was raised by Harald Blue-tooth, king of Denmark, in memory of his parents at some time between 965 and 985, but probably between 983 and 985

slabs in the rich district of Norway which bears that name. It was also for a short time popular in England where it blended with, and perhaps influenced, the later development of the rich and rather lush Winchester style during the reign of Cnut and the other Danish kings of the eleventh century. Ringerike ornament grew naturally in the mid eleventh century into the last truly Viking style – the Urnes style – with its smooth, sinuous fighting animals, which appear in all their decadent perfection on the fascinating reconstructed stave church at Urnes in Norway.

Ills 49, 50

Ill. 106

Ills 107–109

Ill. 108

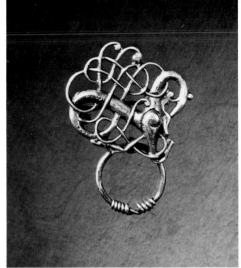

106–108 *Above*, *left*, ornament of the Ringerike style, which is also to be seen in *Ill. 50*, is here shown in an English manuscript, probably painted at Winchcombe, Gloucestershire, in the early years of the eleventh century. *Above*, *right*, a brooch from Lindholm Høje in Denmark, takes the form of an animal of the Urnes style – the final ornamental style of the Viking period. The style, which lasts from the middle of the eleventh to the middle of the twelfth century, takes its name from the Norwegian stave-church at Urnes, the portal of which is shown *left*

This outline of a vital art is intended to explain the sequence of the styles seen in the accompanying illustrations. It is an art which may seem to be vulgar in the way that baroque art is vulgar. The Viking artist could not bear to see an empty space, every square centimetre had to be filled with contorted and coiled creatures. The roots of the art lay in the Germanic past of Scandinavia, and if it ever had any meaning, that meaning had by this time been lost. It had little restraint, and only on the runic *Ills 80–83* memorial stones of Sweden and on one or two other objects decorated in the Urnes style does a certain clean- *Ill. 109* ness of line give it a quality which is almost to the modern taste. Technically this ornament is a fantastic achievement; let us enjoy its technique even if we may not approve its form.

109 A silver bowl from Lilla Valla, Gotland, Sweden, ornamented in a style transitional between Ringerike and Urnes. In Sweden this style and the pure Urnes style occurs on many of the memorial stones of the eleventh century and, for this reason, is sometimes known as the rune-stone style

The Coming of Christianity

Ill. 105

Save in the island of Gotland (where there had been a continuous tradition since the end of the Roman Iron Age) decorative stone carving was unknown in Scandinavia until the middle of the tenth century, when, possibly under English influence, the custom of raising ornamented memorials in stone was initiated. One of the first such stones comes from the Danish royal cemetery at Jelling in Jutland. It is a semi-pyramidal boulder of red-veined granite, rather more than 2½ m. in height; one face bears a lion in the Mammen style caught up in the coils of a snake, the second face a primitive representation of the Crucifixion, while the third face carries an inscription:

> King Harald ordered this stone to be raised in memory of Gorm his father and Thyra his mother. [He was] that Harald who won all Denmark and Norway, and made all the Danes Christian.

The Harald referred to is Harald Bluetooth (940–85) and the stone was probably set up between 983 and 985.

The events which led to the conversion of Denmark in the middle of the tenth century had started much earlier. The first recorded attempt to convert the Danes had been made by the English missionary, Willibrord, in the early years of the eighth century. He met with no success, but brought back with him thirty Danish youths, perhaps with the intention of founding a seminary. Various attempts were made in the following years to convert the Danes, but they generally came to nothing. In the early thirties of the ninth century a German monk, Ansgar, at the behest of the Emperor Louis the Pious, journeyed to Birka in Sweden and converted a fair number of people, including the official representative of the King, a man called Herigar, who built a church on his estate. The missionaries returned to Germany after two years' work among the pagan Swedes. Ansgar, the apostle of Scandinavia, later became Bishop of Hamburg and, after the sack of this town by the Danes in 845, Bishop of Bremen in plurality with Hamburg; from there he founded a church in Schleswig in which many Danes were baptized. Meanwhile the missionaries he had sent to Birka had been expelled – one, Nithard, had been killed – but about 850 Ansgar dispatched a priest to Birka and, some two years later, went there again himself. After a certain amount of initial obstruction he received the support of the King, who bought out of his own pocket a house for one of his missionaries, Erimbert. At all times the missionaries in the North appear to have been treated with tolerance, although there were often short periods of persecution during which a church or mission-station might be closed. The conversion of the North was slow, but was not carried out by force, rather by argument and conviction.

In 935 the break-through came for the Christian missionaries. One of Ansgar's successors as Archbishop of Hamburg and Bremen (Unni) went to Denmark and managed, through Harald Bluetooth the King's son, to get permission to preach throughout Denmark. He then went to Birka only to find that the Swedes had reverted to paganism. It was there that he died in 936. As early as 948 sees were established with German missionary bishops in Denmark at Hedeby, Ribe and Åarhus. Harald became Christian between 960 and 965, probably for political reasons, for at about the same time he submitted to the Emperor Otto I, whom he recognized as overlord.

It was probably about this time that Norway also became influenced by Christianity – Håkon the Good who died c. 960 was a Christian – but it is not until the reign of Olaf Tryggvason, who came to the throne in 995, that Norway officially adopted the new faith – at the point of the sword. This forcible conversion was not very

110 Cast-bronze figure of the Norwegian saint and king Olaf, on the Irish reliquary of Saint Manchan, probably made between 1120 and 1130

Ill. 110 effective, and it was during the reign of St Olaf (1014–30) that the Norwegians were finally converted by both English and German missionaries. Iceland was converted in 1000 by act of the Althing:

> Then it was made law that all people should be Christian and those be baptized who still were unbaptized in this land; but as to exposure of children the old law should stand and also as to eating of horseflesh. People might sacrifice to heathen gods secretly, if they wished, but under penalty of the lesser outlawry if this was proved by witnesses. But a few winters later this heathendom was abolished like the rest.

Sweden, however, was still basically a pagan country and, despite the formal acceptance of Christianity by King Olaf Skötkonung in 1008 and his foundation of the bishopric of Skara, it was probably not until well on into the twelfth century that the Swedes became Christian and the great temple at Uppsala, described by Adam of Bremen, was destroyed.

Conclusion

The Church landed pen in hand and, as the North became part of the literate European Christian community, its vitality was strangely sapped and the Viking Age came to an end. The tenth and eleventh centuries saw the Scandinavian countries at the peak of their international importance; never again were they to make the same impression on European life. Achievements of latter-day Scandinavian heroes of the stamp of Gustavus Adolphus and Charles XII pale into insignificance beside the conquests and explorations of the Vikings. The vital civilization which the classical authors at the beginning of the millennium had only dimly perceived in the Pythean mists had risen like a star to its zenith – an object of wonder and fear to the world of the succeeding millennium.

Select Bibliography

This select list of books is intended partly as a guide to further reading and partly as a list of the more fundamental books concerned with the period covered by this book. To this end I have largely confined my references to books in English, French and German, and only in important cases have I referred to books in Scandinavian languages, many of which have summaries in other languages. Most of the books have extensive bibliographies.

General

ANDERSEN, P.S., *Samlingen av Norge og kristningen av landet*, Oslo 1977.
KLINDT-JENSEN, O., *Denmark before the Vikings*, London 1957.
HAGEN, A., *Norway*, London 1967.
KIVIKOSKI, E., *Finland*, London 1967.
SELLEVOLD, B.J., *et al.*, *Iron Age man in Denmark*, København 1984.
SKOVGAARD-PETERSEN, I., *et al.*, *Danmarks Historie*, i, København 1977.
STENBERGER, M., *Sweden*, London 1963
—— *Det forntida, Sverige*, Stockholm 1964.
WILSON, D.M., (ed.) *The Northern World*, London 1980.

The Roman Iron Age

EGGERS, H.G., *Der römische Import im freien Germanien (Atlas der Urgeschichte, 1)*, Hamburg 1951.
STJERNQUIST, B., *Simris, on cultural connections in the Roman Iron Age*, Lund 1955.
WHEELER, R.E.M., *Rome beyond the Imperial frontiers*, London 1954.

The Migration and Vendel periods

KLINDT-JENSEN, O., *Bornholm i folkevandringstiden*, København 1957.
LAMM, J.P. and NORDSTROM, H.-Å., *Vendel Period Studies*, Stockholm 1983.
SJÖVOLD, T., *The Iron Age Settlement of Arctic Norway*, Tromsö/Oslo 1962.

The Viking Age (General)

FOOTE, P.G., and WILSON, D.M., *The Viking Achievement*, London 1970.
GRAHAM-CAMPBELL, J., and KIDD, D., *The Vikings*, London 1980.
JONES, G., *A history of the Vikings*, new ed., Oxford 1984.
ROESDAHL, E., *Viking Age Denmark*, London 1982.
ROESDAHL, E., *Vikingernes Verden*, København 1987.
SAWYER, P.A., *Kings and Vikings*, London 1982.

Settlement

AMBROSIANI, B., *Fornlämningar och bebyggelse*, Stockholm 1964.
HAGEN, A., *Studier i jernalderens gårdssamfunn*, Oslo 1953.
PETERSEN, J., *Gamle gårdsanlegg i Rogaland*, Oslo 1936.
ROESDAHL, E., 'The Danish geometrical Viking fortresses and their context', *Anglo-Norman Studies*, ix (1987).
STENBERGER, M., (ed.), *Forntida gårdar i Island*, København 1943.
STENBERGER, M. and KLINDT-JENSEN, O., *Vallhagar*, Stockholm 1955.

Art

BAILEY, R.N. *Viking Age Sculpture in northern England*, London 1980.
BERG, K., *et al.*, *Norges kunsthistorie*, i, Oslo 1981.
FUGLESANG, S.H., *Some Aspects of the Ringerike Style*, Odense 1980.
HOLMQVIST, W., *Germanic Art*, Stockholm 1955.
SALIN, B., *Die altgermanische Thierornamentik*, Stockholm 1904.
WILSON, D.M. and KLINDT-JENSEN, O., *Viking Art*, London 1966.

Pagan gods, Christianity and religion

TURVILLE-PETRE, E.O.G., *Myth and Religion of the North*, London 1964.
OLSEN, O., 'Hørg, Hov og Kirke', *Aarbøger for nordisk oldkyndighed og historie*, 1965.
SAWYER, B., *et al.* (ed.) *The Christianization of Scandinavia*, Alingsås 1987.

Sacrificial offerings

ENGLEHARDT, C., *Denmark in the Early Iron Age*, London 1866.
HAGBERG, U.E., *The archaeology of Skedemosse*, Stockholm 1967.
MÜLLER-WILLE, M., 'Operplätze der Wikingerzeit' *Frühmittelalterliche Studien*, XVIII (1984).
STJERNQUIST, B., 'Präliminarien zu einer Untersuchung von Opferfunden', *Meddelanden från Lunds universitets historiska museum*, 1962–3, 5–64.

Runes

JANSSON, S.B.F., *Runes in Sweden*, Stockholm 1987.
MOLTKE, E., *Runes and their origin*, Copenhagen 1985.

Viking graves

ARBMAN, H., *Birka I*, Stockholm 1940.
BERSU, G. and WILSON, D.M., *Three Viking graves in the Isle of Man*, London 1966.
BRØNDSTED, J., 'Danish inhumation graves of the Viking Age' *Acta Archaeologica*, VII (1936), 81–228.
GRÄSLUND, A.-S., *Birka IV, The burial customs*, Uppsala 1980.
RAMSKOU, T., 'Viking Age Cremation Graves in Denmark', *Acta Archaeologica*, XXI (1950), 137–182.

STRÖMBERG, M., *Untersuchungen zur jüngeren Eisenzeit in Schonen*, Lund 1961.

The Vikings in western Europe and Britain

ARBMAN, H. and STENBERGER, M., *Vikingar i Västerled*, Stockholm 1935.
BATES, D., *Normandy before 1066*, London 1982.
CRAWFORD, B.E., *Scandinavian Scotland*, Leicester 1987.
ROESDAHL, E., *et al.* (ed.), *The Vikings in England*, London 1981.
SHETELIG, H., *Viking Antiquities in Great Britain and Ireland*, Oslo 1940–54.

The Vikings in the East

ARBMAN, H., *Svear i österviking*, Stockholm 1955.
GREKOV, B.G., *Kiev Rus*, Moscow 1959.
HANNESTAD, K. (ed.), *Varangian Problems, Scando-Slavica*, Supp. i, 1970.
STENDER-PETERSEN, A., *Varangica*, Århus 1953.
VERNADSKY, G., *The origins of Russia*, Oxford 1959.

The Vikings in the North Atlantic

ELDJÁRN, K., *Kuml og Haugfé úr heiðnum sið í Íslandi*, Akureyri 1956.
JONES, G., *The Norse Atlantic Saga*, Oxford 1964.
KROGH, K.J., *Viking Greenland*, Copenhagen 1967.
MAGNUSSON, M. and PÁLSSON, H., *The Vinland Sagas*, Harmondsworth 1965.
WAHLGREN, E., *The Vikings and America*, London 1986.

Ships

BINNS, A., *Viking Voyagers. Then and now*, London 1980.
BRØGGER, A.W. and SHETELIG, H., *The Viking Ships, their ancestry and evolution*, Oslo 1951.
OLSEN, O. and CRUMLIN-PEDERSEN, O., *Five Viking Ships from Roskilde Fjord*, Copenhagen 1978.

Towns and trading stations

ARBMAN, H., *Birka, Sveriges äldsta handelstad*, Stockholm 1939.
BENCARD, M. (ed.), *Ribe Excavations 1970–76*, Esbjerg 1981–.
BRADLEY, J., (ed.), *Viking Dublin Exposed*, Dublin 1984.
HALL, R. (ed.), *The Viking Dig. The excavations at York*, London 1984.
HOLMQVIST, W., *et al.*, *Excavations at Helgö*, Stockholm 1961 (in progress).
JANKUHN, H., *Haithabu, ein Handelsplatz der Wikingerzeit*, 8th ed., Neumünster 1986.
—— *Berichte über die Ausgrabungen in Haithabu*, i (1969)–.

Coins and hoards of the Viking period

BLACKBURN, M.A.S. and METCALF, D.M. (ed.), *Viking Age Coinage in northern lands*, Oxford 1981.

GRIEG, S., 'Vikingetidens skattefund', *Universitetets Oldsaksamlings Skrifter*, ii (1929), 177–312.

MALMER, B., *Nordiska mynt före år 1000*, Lund 1966.

SKOVMAND, R., 'De danske Skattefund fra Vikingetiden', *Aarbøger for nordisk oldkyndighed og historie*, 1942, 1–275.

STENBERGER, M., *Die Schatzfunde Gotlands der Wikingerzeit*, Stockholm 1947–58.

Daily Life

GRAHAM-CAMPBELL, J., *Viking Artefacts, a select catalogue*, London 1980.

HALD, M., *Jernalderens Dragt*, København 1962.

PETERSEN, J., *Vikingetidens Redskaper*, Oslo 1951.

Literature and chronicles

Most of the writing concerning the literature of the north is in Scandinavian languages and the texts are naturally published in their original tongue. General surveys of Icelandic literature in English will be found in S. Einarsson, *A history of Icelandic literature* (New York 1957), and G. Turville-Petre, *Origins of Icelandic Literature* (Oxford 1953). Many sagas and other historical documents have been translated into English and the reader is referred to editions published by Penguin, Oxford University Press, Messrs Nelson and Messrs Dent (in the *Everyman* series). The translations by William Morris and Magnusson are still worth reading. *Islendingabók* has been translated by H. Hermansson (New York 1930), *Landnámabók* by G. Vigfusson and F. York Powell in *Origines Islandicae*, I, 1905. The reader is also referred to the books by Jones and by Magnusson and Pálsson in the section 'The Vikings in the north Atlantic' above. For foreign sources see *The Primary Russian Chronicle*, translated by S.H. Cross and O.P. Sherbowitz-Wetzor (Cambridge, Mass. 1953). English sources translated by D. Whitelock, *English Historical Documents*, 2nd ed. London 1980, the *Vita Anskari*, translated by C.H. Robinson in *Anskar, The Apostle of the North* (London 1921); the Anglo-Saxon epic *Beowulf* is translated by E. Talbot Donaldson (London 1966). H. Zettel, *Das Bild der Normannen under der Normanneneinfälle in westfränkischen, ostfränkischen und angelsächsischen Quellen des 8. bis 11. jahrhunderts* (München 1977), is a good critical discussion of the western historical sources for the Viking Age. Constantine Porphyrogenitos' *de administrando imperio* is translated by R.J.H. Jenkins (Budapest/London 1949–62).

Periodical and serial publications

The following journals publish archaeological material in English, French and German: *Acta Archaeologica, Kuml, Meddenlanden från Lunds universitets historiska museum, Medieval Scandinavia* and *Norwegian Archaeological Review*. Journals with summaries in western languages are *Viking, Aarbøger for nordisk oldkyndighed og historie, Universitetets Oldsaksamlings Skrifter, Fornvännen* and *Tor*. A useful guide to vast areas of Scandinavia is *Kulturhistorisk Leksikon for nordisk middelalder*, 1956–78, which is published in Scandinavian languages without a summary. An important English publication is the *Saga Book of the Viking Society for Northern Research*. The *Proceedings* of the various Viking Congresses are an important source of interdisciplinary work since 1949. The annual *Bibliography of Old Norse – Icelandic Studies* has, since 1963, listed all important publications, with a particular bias towards literature and history. Scandinavian historical periodicals tend to be published in the language of the country of origin of the author.

List of Illustrations

The author and publishers are grateful to the many official bodies, institutions and individuals mentioned below for their assistance in supplying illustration material. Illustrations without acknowledgment are from original material in the archives of Thames and Hudson. *ATA* = Antikvarisk Topografiska Arkivet, Stockholm. *NMC* = National Museum, Copenhagen. Museum photo. *SHM* = Statens Historiska Museum, Stockholm. *EW* = copyright Eva Wilson.

Index

The characters ä, å, á are treated as a, æ as ae, ö and ø as o, ð as d, and þ as th. The illustrations are indexed by numbers in *italics*.